SUPER FAST READING

ULTIMATE BOOK FOR READING SPEED

MIGANG PATIR

Made with ♥ on the Notion Press Platform
www.notionpress.com

Contents

Contents

Unlock Your Most Powerful Skill

How much could you achieve if you could learn twice as fast? What if the mountain of books on your nightstand, the endless reports for work, or the dense textbooks for your exams could be conquered in a fraction of the time—while understanding and remembering more?

In our modern world, we are drowning in information but starved for knowledge. The ability to process written content quickly, efficiently, and effectively is no longer a nice-to-have skill; it is a critical superpower for students, professionals, and lifelong learners alike. This is the power of true speed reading—and it is a power that is within your grasp.

Why I Wrote This Book

I wrote Super Fast Reading because for years, I watched brilliant, ambitious people struggle under the weight of their reading lists. They believed they were slow readers, that their focus was weak, or that retaining complex information was a talent they simply didn't possess. I knew this wasn't true. Speed reading is not an innate gift; it is a trainable set of techniques rooted in science and practice.

My goal was to move beyond the hype and create the most comprehensive, practical, and scientifically-grounded guide available. This book demystifies the process, breaks it down into achievable steps, and provides a clear path from your current reading speed to the rapid, proficient level you desire.

Who This Book Is For

This book is for you if:

You are a student facing overwhelming reading assignments and want to study smarter, not harder.

You are a professional who needs to stay on top of industry trends, reports, and emails without it consuming your entire day.

You are a lifelong learner with a passion for books and a desire to absorb more wisdom in your limited free time.

You are anyone who has ever felt frustrated, slow, or distracted while reading and believed you could do better.

How to Use This Book Effectively

Super Fast Reading is designed as a practical workshop in book form. It is not meant to be passively consumed. Here's how to get the most out of it:

Start with the Baseline Test: Begin with Chapter 2 to measure your current reading speed. This is your starting point, and tracking your progress from here will be incredibly motivating.

Understand the 'Why': Chapters 3 and 4 explore the science and mindset behind speed reading. Understanding how your brain and eyes work will make the techniques that follow feel logical and natural.

Practice, Practice, Practice: The core of this book is the exercises in Chapters 5 through 13. Commit to doing them. You wouldn't expect to build muscle by reading about push-ups; you must do them. The same is true for training your reading muscles.

Apply the Strategies: Later chapters show you how to adapt these techniques to different materials, from digital screens to dense academic texts. Use the daily and weekly practice plans in Chapter 16 to build a lasting habit.

Be Patient and Consistent: You will not triple your speed overnight. But with consistent practice, you will see measurable, life-changing improvement week after week.

This book is the culmination of years of research, teaching, and learning from the best minds in cognitive science and accelerated learning. My deepest gratitude goes to the researchers and educators whose work provided the foundation for these techniques.

A special thank you to my students and early readers, whose feedback and success stories shaped this book into its most effective form. And finally, to my family, for their unwavering patience and support during the countless hours spent writing and refining this manuscript.

Your reading journey is about to accelerate dramatically. Turn the page, and let's begin.

Acknowledgements

This book is the culmination of years of research, teaching, and learning from the best minds in cognitive science and accelerated learning. My deepest gratitude goes to the researchers and educators whose work provided the foundation for these techniques.

A special thank you to my students and early readers, whose feedback and success stories shaped this book into its most effective form. And finally, to my family, for their unwavering patience and support during the countless hours spent writing and refining this manuscript.

Your reading journey is about to accelerate dramatically. Turn the page, and let's begin.

The Pile of Unread Books

It started, as it often does, with a pile of books.

It sat on my nightstand—a teetering, silent monument to my own limitations. There was the bestselling business book everyone was quoting, the classic novel I'd always meant to read, the dense history text for a project I was passionate about, and the latest scientific discoveries that felt essential to understanding the world. Each one was a door to a new room of knowledge, a new perspective, a new skill.

And I couldn't get through any of them.

Every night, I'd pick one up with the best intentions. I'd read a page, then my mind would wander to a deadline I was anxious about. I'd read a paragraph, then my eyes would drift back to the same sentence three times, my inner voice dutifully sounding out each word at a plodding, conversational pace. I'd check my progress: twenty pages in forty minutes. At this rate, that one book would take me weeks. The pile might as well have been a mountain.

I felt a familiar frustration, a sinking feeling that I was being left behind. Information was accelerating all around me, a relentless river of text in emails, articles, reports, and messages. I was trying to drink from a firehose with a thimble. I was a lifelong learner who no longer had the time to learn.

This wasn't just about reading faster. It was about keeping up. It was about reclaiming time. It was about the quiet shame of that unread pile and the vibrant, knowledgeable person I wanted to be—the one who could discuss the latest ideas, master new subjects quickly, and still have time to live a life outside the pages.

My quest began out of sheer necessity. I devoured every article, study, and old book on speed reading I could find. I was skeptical. The promises seemed outlandish—double your speed, triple it, with perfect comprehension? It sounded like a late-night infomercial. But the science, when I dug into it, was compelling. It wasn't magic; it was mechanics. It was about understanding how the brain and eyes work together (and sometimes work against each other) and then systematically training them to perform better.

I became my own test subject. I practiced eye exercises until I felt silly. I used a pointer to guide my vision across the page. I learned to quiet the subvocalization in my head and to see groups of words instead of individual ones. It was awkward at first. It felt forced. But then, something incredible happened.

The mechanics faded into the background, and the meaning rushed to the foreground.

The words stopped being marks on a page and started becoming direct streams of ideas. The pile on my nightstand began to shrink. Not because I was spending every waking moment reading, but because I was reading differently. I was efficient. I was focused. I was in control. The mountain became manageable, then it became molehills. The frustration was replaced by a profound sense of power and possibility.

This book is the map of that journey. It is the collection of every effective technique, every scientific insight, and every practical exercise I learned and refined along the way. It is the guide I wish I'd had when I stared at that daunting pile, feeling behind and overwhelmed.

The journey to becoming a super fast reader is not just about technical proficiency. It is a shift in identity. It is moving from seeing yourself as a slow, easily distracted reader to knowing yourself as a capable, efficient, and powerful learner.

That pile of books is waiting. Let's start reading.

Migang Patir

1

Unlocking the Power of Your Mind – An Introduction to Speed Reading

We live in the Information Age, a time of unprecedented access to knowledge. Every day, we are bombarded with a deluge of words: emails, reports, articles, books, social media updates. This constant stream is both a blessing and a curse. While we have the world's knowledge at our fingertips, we are also faced with a pervasive and modern anxiety: **information overload.**

The feeling is universal. The stack of books on your nightstand grows faster than you can read them. Your "Read It Later" app becomes a digital graveyard of good intentions. The crucial document for work sits unread, its density daunting. We are all reading more than ever before, yet we feel we are understanding and retaining less. We skim, we scroll, we multitask, and in doing so, we sacrifice depth for breadth, comprehension for completion.

But what if there was a better way? What if you could not only keep pace with the torrent of information but master it? What if you could read a book in a single sitting, remember the key points of a complex report with ease, and finally conquer that ever-growing reading list—all while understanding more and enjoying the process?

This is not a fantasy. This is the promise of speed reading.

This book is your guide to fulfilling that promise. It is a practical, science-backed manual designed to transform your relationship with reading from one of stress and obligation to one of confidence, efficiency, and profound enjoyment. We begin our journey here, by laying a solid foundation: understanding what speed reading truly is, how it works, and why it is one of the most impactful skills you will ever acquire.

What is Speed Reading? A Clear Definition

Let's dispel the Hollywood image of pages flipping in a blur, with a reader absorbing every word through some form of osmosis. Speed reading is not magic. It is a set of learnable techniques and cognitive strategies designed to optimize the reading process for maximum efficiency and comprehension.

A more accurate definition:

Speed reading is the ability to recognize and absorb phrases or sentences with a single glance (fixation), significantly reducing the time and cognitive effort required to process text, while maintaining or even improving comprehension and retention.

The core of this definition is **efficiency.** You are not learning to see words faster; you are learning to process them more intelligently. You are replacing inefficient, subconscious habits with purposeful, trained techniques. It is the difference between taking a meandering, scenic route to a destination and taking a direct highway. You arrive at the same place—understanding the text—but you do so far more quickly and with less wasted energy.

The Science Behind Fast Reading: How Your Brain Processes Text

To improve your reading, you must first understand the machinery. Reading is a complex neurological dance between your eyes and your brain, and its bottlenecks are well understood by science.

The Eye-Brain Connection: Reading is not a smooth, camera-like scan of a page. Your eyes move in quick, jerky movements called saccades. Between each saccade, your eyes stop for a fraction of a second to take a "picture" of the text. This stop is called a fixation. It is only during these fixations that actual reading occurs.

The Bottlenecks of the Average Reader:

Too Many Fixations: An untrained reader makes fixations on nearly every single word, or even on parts of longer words. This is like taking multiple pictures of a landscape when one wide-angle shot would suffice.

Subvocalization: This is the inner voice in your head that "says" the words as you read. While it can be useful for poetry or complex texts, it acts as a governor on your reading speed, limiting you to the pace of speech (around 150-250 words per minute). Your brain is capable of understanding ideas far faster than your mouth can speak them.

Regression: This is the habit of unconsciously skipping back to re-read words or sentences you've already passed. While sometimes necessary for complex material, it is often just a habit that destroys rhythm and flow, adding significant time to your reading.

Speed reading techniques are designed to overcome these specific bottlenecks:

Widening the Perceptual Span: Training your peripheral vision to take in more words per fixation (e.g., reading "the quick brown fox" as a single chunk instead of four separate words).

Minimizing Subvocalization: Learning to recognize words and phrases visually and conceptually, bypassing the need to "hear" them internally.

Eliminating Regression: Using a visual guide to pace your eyes forward consistently, training your brain to trust its initial comprehension.

Common Myths vs. Facts: Separating Hype from Reality

The field of speed reading is often shrouded in mystery and exaggerated by sensational claims. To embark on this journey with clarity and confidence, it is essential to dispel the most common misconceptions and replace them with evidence-based truths.

Myth 1: Speed Reading is Just Fancy Skimming.

This is perhaps the most pervasive and damaging myth. People often equate moving one's eyes quickly across a page with the deliberate, strategic process of speed reading.

The Fact: Skimming and speed reading are distinct skills with different purposes. Skimming is a surface-level technique used to preview text or extract only the main ideas and gist. It involves intentionally skipping large portions of the material. True speed reading, however, aims for full comprehension of the entire text. The goal is not to omit information but to process it more efficiently. You are reading every crucial word, but you are doing so by absorbing groups of words at a time, thereby eliminating the inefficiencies that slow down traditional reading.

Myth 2: Superhuman Speeds of 10,000+ Words Per Minute are Possible.

Extravagant claims of reading entire novels in minutes have captured the public imagination, often fueled by stage performers and misleading marketing.

The Fact: Neurological science places a firm upper limit on reading speed with full comprehension. The human brain and eyes are simply not wired to process and comprehend complex information at such astronomical rates. Claims of speeds beyond roughly 500-800 words per minute for dense material often refer to "visual paging" or selective keyword spotting—useful skills in their own right, but they are not equivalent to the deep, contextual understanding that defines reading. This book focuses on achievable, sustainable speeds that will double or triple your current rate while radically improving your grasp of the material.

Myth 3: You Must Sacrifice Comprehension and Enjoyment for Speed.
Many fear that reading faster will turn the serene pleasure of getting lost in a book into a frantic, stressful race to the finish line, leaving understanding in the dust.
The Fact: The opposite is typically true. The techniques you will learn—such as improved focus, reduced regression, and active engagement with the text—are proven to enhance comprehension. By eliminating the mental drift and subconscious re-reading that plague slow readers, your mind becomes more focused and better able to absorb and connect ideas. Furthermore, the frustration of a slow, plodding pace is replaced by the flow state and confidence of efficient reading, which dramatically increases enjoyment and reduces mental fatigue.

Myth 4: It's Only Useful for Light Reading Like Novels or News.
Some believe these techniques are only applicable to simple, narrative-driven texts and fall apart when faced with a dense textbook or technical manual.
The Fact: While it is true that you will naturally adjust your pace based on the complexity of the material, the core principles of speed reading are universally beneficial. For difficult texts, the strategies of pre-reading, chunking, and focused attention become even more critical. You will learn to navigate complex information more strategically, identifying key arguments and evidence quickly, which allows you to allocate your time and mental energy to the most challenging sections. It makes tackling difficult material less daunting and more efficient.

Myth 5: You Have to Be a Naturally Fast Reader to Benefit.
This myth suggests that speed reading is an innate talent, a gift bestowed on a select few, and not a skill that can be developed by the average person.
The Fact: Speed reading is a learned skill, much like learning to type or play a musical instrument. It is not dependent on natural talent or a high IQ. Anyone who can read can learn to read more efficiently. It requires understanding a set of principles and, most

importantly, consistent and mindful practice to overcome ingrained habits. This book is designed to guide anyone, regardless of their starting point, through that process of transformation.

Why Speed Reading is a Life-Changing Skill

Mastering this skill extends far beyond simply getting through your inbox faster. It is a fundamental upgrade to your cognitive toolkit that impacts every area of your life.

Professional Dominance: Imagine being the person who can quickly synthesize a 50-page industry report, stay on top of the latest trends, and prepare for meetings with unparalleled thoroughness. Speed reading gives you a significant competitive advantage.

Academic Excellence: For students, the ability to process vast quantities of required reading efficiently is a game-changer. It reduces stress, frees up time for deeper study and revision, and leads to better grades.

Lifelong Learning: With an efficient reading engine, the pursuit of knowledge becomes a joy, not a burden. You can explore new subjects, delve into history, understand complex philosophies, and continuously grow your expertise throughout your life.

Reclaimed Time: This is perhaps the most valuable benefit. If you read for just two hours a week and double your speed, you effectively reclaim one entire waking day of your life every single month. That is time you can spend with family, on hobbies, or simply resting.

Enhanced Cognitive Function: The focused concentration required for speed reading is a workout for your brain. It strengthens your attention span, improves your memory, and enhances your ability to think critically and make connections between ideas.

What This Book Will Teach You: A Roadmap to Mastery

This book is designed as a progressive journey. We will start with the fundamentals and build towards advanced, integrated mastery.

The Foundation: We will begin by assessing your current reading habits and speed. Then, we'll dive into the core mechanics: training your eyes to move more efficiently and quieting the inner voice of subvocalization.

Building Comprehension: Speed is useless without understanding. Here, you will learn powerful pre-reading strategies, techniques for active engagement with the text, and methods to dramatically improve your retention and recall.

Advanced Techniques & Application: We will explore how to adapt your speed to different materials, from dense nonfiction to flowing fiction. You'll learn to tackle digital reading, develop a personal reading system, and integrate note-taking and knowledge management.

Sustaining the Practice: Mastery is a long-term pursuit. This section provides strategies for overcoming obstacles, building unbreakable focus, creating a lifelong reading habit, and using the tools and resources that will support your journey.

The path to becoming a master reader is before you. It requires an open mind and a willingness to practice, but the rewards are immense. You are about to unlock one of the most profound capabilities of your mind. Turn the page, and let's begin.

2

Laying the Groundwork – Requirements for the Exercises

❦

Embarking on the journey to master speed reading is like training for a marathon. You wouldn't attempt to run 26 miles without the right shoes, a training plan, and a proper warm-up. Similarly, effective speed reading requires the right tools, environment, and mindset. Without these foundational elements, practice becomes inefficient, and progress stalls. This chapter will equip you with everything you need to begin your training effectively, ensuring that the time you invest in the subsequent exercises yields maximum returns.

1. Tools Needed

Having the right tools at your disposal removes friction and allows you to focus purely on the technique. Here's what you'll need:

Your Finger or a Pen: This is your most crucial tool, acting as a **pacer**. Your eyes are naturally drawn to movement. By gliding your finger or pen underneath the line you're reading, you guide your eyes smoothly, preventing regression (skip-back) and encouraging a faster, more consistent rhythm. It forces your eyes to follow a set pace.

Printed Text for Beginners: While digital speed reading is a valuable skill, **start with physical, printed materials**. A book or printed article provides a tactile, consistent format without screen glare, notifications, or the temptation to click away. It allows you to easily use your pacer and practice techniques like meta-guiding.

Digital Device (for later stages): Once you are comfortable with the techniques on paper, transition to practicing on a tablet, e-reader, or computer. Use apps or browser extensions that are designed for speed reading (e.g., those that use RSVP - Rapid Serial Visual Presentation). This is essential for applying your skills to the digital content you consume daily.

A Timer: Your smartphone timer is perfect for this. You will use it to consistently measure your reading speed (Words Per Minute - WPM) to track your progress objectively.

A Practice Book or Material: As emphasized, you need dedicated material you are willing to mark up and read multiple times. This book provides articles for this purpose. The key is to use text you are familiar with for practice drills, separating the goal of learning technique from the goal of learning new content.

2. Best Environment for Practice

Creating a dedicated space signals to your brain that it's time to focus. A distracted mind cannot learn new, demanding skills.

Lighting: Ensure your reading space is **brightly** lit to reduce eye strain. Natural light is ideal, but a good desk lamp that illuminates the page without creating a glare on the paper or screen is essential. The light source should come from behind you, not shine directly into your eyes or reflect off your reading material.

Posture: Sit upright at a desk or table. Avoid reading lying down or in a overly relaxed chair. Good posture promotes alertness and improves blood flow, keeping your mind sharp and your field of vision optimal for taking in lines of text.

Minimizing Distractions:

Digital: This is non-negotiable. Turn off notifications on your phone and computer. Better yet, put your phone on silent and place it in another room. If practicing on a computer, close all unrelated browser tabs and applications.

Physical: Find a quiet, tidy space. A cluttered desk can lead to a cluttered mind. Use a "Do Not Disturb" sign if necessary to ensure uninterrupted practice sessions.

Time: Identify your "prime time"—the time of day when you are naturally most alert and focused (e.g., first thing in the morning, or during a quiet afternoon). Schedule your practice sessions for these periods.

3. The Inner Tools: Mindset and Health

Your physical and mental state are the engines of your progress.

Positive Attitude & Perseverance: Approach this skill with the pragmatic optimism of a scientist. You are experimenting and practicing. Some days you will see massive gains; other days, it may feel difficult. Understand that, like any skill, this requires **perseverance**. Trust the process outlined in this book. Your self-belief is the fuel that will get you through the challenging phases of practice.

Sound Health: Your brain is a physical organ. Adequate sleep, proper nutrition, and hydration are not optional; they are prerequisites for cognitive performance. A tired, under-fueled brain cannot maintain the high levels of concentration required for speed reading.

Focused Attention: Speed reading is an active sport for your mind. It requires single-tasking. You must commit to avoiding multitasking entirely during your practice sessions. The goal is to train your cognitive resources on one thing: reading efficiently. Remember, the ability to focus is a muscle that gets stronger with use.

4. Setting Realistic Goals

Unrealistic expectations are the fastest way to discouragement. Howard Berg's 25,000 WPM is the Olympic gold medal of speed reading—it's an inspiration, not a starting point.

Aim for Gradual Improvement: A realistic and excellent goal is to **double your original reading speed** while maintaining or even improving your comprehension. If you start at 250 WPM, aiming for 500 WPM is a fantastic achievement.

Focus on Consistency, Not Perfection: Your goal for each session should not be to break a record, but to consistently practice the techniques for a set amount of time (e.g., 15-20 minutes daily).

Celebrate Milestones: When you see a 50 WPM increase, celebrate it! These small wins provide motivation to continue.

5. Measuring Your Current Reading Speed (Baseline Test)

You cannot manage what you do not measure. Establishing your baseline is critical for tracking progress. Here's how to do it:

Select a Test Passage: Choose a typical, non-fiction book or article you have not read before. It should be at a moderate difficulty level. This book includes standardized passages for this purpose.

Count the Words: Count the number of words in exactly 10 lines. Divide this number by 10 to get the average words-per-line. Then, count the total number of lines in the passage and multiply by your average words-per-line to get the total word count. (Note: For the practice passages in this book, the word count is provided for you.)

Time Yourself: Use your timer. Read the passage at your normal reading pace with the goal of understanding the content. When you start reading, start the timer. When you finish, stop it.

Calculate Your WPM: Use the following formula:

Words Per Minute (WPM) = (Total Word Count / Time in Seconds) * 60

Test Your Comprehension: Immediately after reading, write down a few bullet points summarizing what you just read. Or, have a friend ask you 3-5 specific questions about the text. Your ability to recall the information is a baseline for your comprehension rate.

Record this baseline WPM and comprehension score. This is your starting point. You will repeat this test with new, unfamiliar passages every week to objectively measure your improvement.

By securing the right tools, environment, and mindset, and by setting a clear baseline, you have built a solid foundation for mastery. You are now ready to begin the practical work of training your eyes and mind to read at an accelerated pace.

3

The Science of Speed Reading: Rewiring Your Brain to Read Faster

Speed reading often feels like a superpower, but it is not magic. It is a science. It is the conscious application of techniques that align with—and optimize—the natural way your brain and eyes process information. To truly master these techniques, you must first understand the machinery you are trying to upgrade. This chapter delves into the fascinating neuroscience and cognitive psychology behind reading. We will explore the bottlenecks that slow you down and the proven methods to bypass them, transforming you from a passive reader into an active information processor.

1. How the Brain Processes Words and Meaning

Reading is a remarkably recent invention in human history, and our brains have not evolved a dedicated "reading center." Instead, we repurpose existing neural networks designed for object recognition and language processing.

13

The Two Pathways: When you read a word, your brain engages in a complex dance between two key regions:

The Visual Cortex: Located at the back of your brain, this area first perceives the word as a visual object—a unique pattern of lines and curves.

Language Centers (Broca's and Wernicke's Areas): Primarily in the left hemisphere, these areas are responsible for speech production and comprehension. The visual pattern is sent here to be linked to its sound (phonology) and its meaning (semantics).

From Symbols to Meaning: The ultimate goal of reading is not to "hear" every word in your head but to access meaning directly. Fluent readers begin to recognize common words and phrases as single units (or "chunks"), much like recognizing a friend's face instantly without analyzing every feature. This direct route from visual form to meaning is the highway speed reading aims to travel.

2. Eye Movement: Fixations, Saccades, and Regressions

Your eyes do not glide smoothly across a line of text like a scanner. They move in a series of rapid, jerky movements called **saccades**, punctuated by brief pauses called **fixations**.

Fixations: This is where reading actually happens. During a fixation, which lasts about 200-250 milliseconds, your eyes stop and your brain takes a "snapshot" of the text within your focus. The average reader fixates on almost every single word, sometimes even on small words like "a" or "the."

Saccades: These are the lightning-fast jumps your eyes make between fixations, lasting about 20-40 milliseconds. During a saccade, you are effectively **blind**. Your brain suppresses visual input to prevent a blurry mess; it's too busy planning the next jump.

The Perceptual Span: During each fixation, you can actually perceive more than just the single word you're focused on. Your **perceptual span** extends 3-4 letters to the left of the fixation point and about 14-15 letters to the right. This is your peripheral vision for reading. Speed reading techniques train you to widen your effective use of this span.

Regressions (Skip-Backs): These are backward saccades where your eyes jump back to re-read a word or phrase. Sometimes this is a conscious choice to understand a complex idea. Often, however, it is an unconscious habit driven by doubt, lack of focus, or poor pacing. Regressions can account for up to 30% of a slow reader's reading time, making them a major target for elimination.

The Science in Action: Imagine a slow reader's eye movement pattern looks like this:

The -> quick -> brown -> fox -> jumps -> over -> the -> lazy -> dog.
(9 fixations, plus potential regressions)

A speed reader's goal is to make it look like this:
The quick brown -> fox jumps over -> the lazy dog.
(3 fixations, no regressions)

3. Subvocalization: The Inner Narrator That Slows You Down

Subvocalization is the internal speech you "hear" in your mind as you read. It involves subtle, unconscious movements of the muscles in your throat and tongue.

Why We Do It: It's a vestige of how we learned to read aloud as children. This inner narrator helps with comprehension and memory for beginners by linking visual symbols to their auditory counterparts.

Why It's a Bottleneck: The problem is that your inner narrator has a speed limit. The average speaking pace is around 150-250 words per minute (WPM). If you subvocalize every word, you are **chaining your reading speed to your speaking speed**. This is the single greatest physiological constraint that prevents you from reading faster.

The Goal is Reduction, Not Elimination: It is a myth that you must eliminate subvocalization entirely. For complex technical material or beautiful prose, you may want to "hear" it. The goal of speed reading is to reduce unnecessary subvocalization. You learn to recognize words and phrases visually without needing to "say" them internally, reserving inner speech for key concepts or difficult passages.

How to Bypass It: Using a pacer (your finger/pen) forces your eyes to move faster than your inner voice can keep up. Over time, your brain adapts and learns to trust the visual processing pathway without needing the auditory crutch for every word.

4. Balancing Speed with Comprehension: The Ultimate Goal

The greatest fear about reading faster is that understanding will plummet. This is a valid concern if speed is pursued recklessly. However, scientific studies show that with proper technique, the relationship between speed and comprehension is not a simple trade-off; it can be a synergistic loop.

The "Sweet Spot": Research indicates that for many readers, **moderate increases in speed can actually improve comprehension**. Why? Because reading too slowly allows your mind to wander. You lose the thread of the argument, get bogged down in insignificant details, and forget the beginning of a sentence by the time you reach the end. A faster pace keeps your brain engaged and focused on the core narrative or argument.

The Comprehension Curve: Imagine a curve. At very slow speeds, comprehension is good but time efficiency is poor. As speed increases, comprehension initially rises due to improved focus, reaching an optimal peak. Beyond this peak, if speed is increased too much without skill, comprehension will indeed drop off as the brain becomes overloaded.

Active Reading Enhances Comprehension: Speed reading is not passive skimming. It is an **active search for meaning**. You are constantly looking for key words, thematic statements, and structural signposts (like "however," "therefore," "in conclusion"). This active engagement often leads to a deeper and more efficient understanding of the text's structure and main ideas than a passive, word-by-word reading would.

Adjusting Your Pace: A skilled speed reader is like a skilled driver: they adjust their speed based on the conditions. You might speed read a novel or a news article, but slow down to analyze a legal contract or a complex scientific formula. **The skill lies in knowing how and when to shift gears**. The techniques you are learning give you the tools to read at 600, 800, or 1000 WPM when appropriate, not the obligation to do so all the time.

Conclusion: The science reveals that traditional reading is inefficient not because of a brain limitation, but because of ingrained habits. Your brain is capable of processing information at astonishing speeds. By understanding the roles of fixation, subvocalization, and active comprehension, you can consciously override these habits. You are not learning to read differently; you are learning to use your brain's inherent capabilities more efficiently. In the next chapter, we will put this science into practice with the core techniques that will redefine your relationship with the written word.

4

Mindset and Preparation: The Inner Game of Speed Reading

⟶ ♡ ⟵

Before a single technique can be mastered, the battlefield must be prepared. That battlefield is your mind. Speed reading is as much a psychological discipline as it is a visual one. The most sophisticated reading methods will fail if your focus is scattered, if you harbor secret beliefs that you "can't do it," or if your motivation fizzles out after a few days. This chapter is dedicated to the inner game. We will equip you with the mental tools to build laser-like focus, dismantle the limiting beliefs that hold you back, cultivate unshakable motivation, and harness the principles of positive psychology to make your learning journey not just effective, but enjoyable and transformative.

1. Building Focus and Concentration: The Mental Muscle

In the digital age, focus is an endangered resource. Reading, especially speed reading, is a profound act of resistance against a world designed to distract you. Building concentration is like building a muscle—it requires consistent training and the right exercises.

The Physiology of Focus: Focus is governed primarily by the prefrontal cortex, the brain's "executive center." This region is energy-intensive and easily fatigued. Understanding this helps you be compassionate with yourself when focus wanes and strategic in how you train it.

The "Third World Ruling" Revisited: As mentioned earlier, this is the tyranny of uncontrolled, intrusive thoughts. To defeat it, you must be proactive:

Pre-Session Mindfulness: Before you begin a practice session, spend 60 seconds in mindfulness. Close your eyes, take three deep breaths, and notice the sounds around you without judgment. This acts as a "mental reset," clearing the RAM of your brain.

The "Not Now" List: If an important but unrelated thought arises during reading (e.g., "I need to call John"), gently acknowledge it—"That's important"—and then defer it. Have a notepad beside you to jot it down in under three seconds. This act of externalizing the thought tells your brain it's safe to let it go for now.

The Pomodoro Technique: Work with your brain's natural rhythm. Set a timer for 25 minutes of intensely focused practice. Then, take a mandatory 5-minute break to walk, stretch, or look out a window. This prevents mental burnout and makes sustained focus manageable.

2. Eliminating Limiting Beliefs About Reading

Your beliefs about your abilities create your reality. These beliefs are often subconscious narratives formed in childhood that now govern your performance. We must bring them into the light and challenge them.

Common Limiting Beliefs:

"I'm a slow reader. It's just how I am." (Fixed Mindset)

"If I read faster, I won't understand or remember anything." (Fear of Loss)

"This is only for geniuses / young people / naturally gifted readers." (Imposter Syndrome)

"I've tried before and failed, so I'll never be able to do it." (Generalization from Past Failure)

The Cognitive Restructuring Process:

Identify: Notice the negative thought when it arises. "I'm never going to get this."

Challenge: Ask yourself, "Is this 100% true? What is the evidence against it?" (e.g., "I have learned difficult things before. My baseline test shows I can already read and comprehend.").

Reframe: Replace the limiting belief with an empowering, truthful statement.

Instead of: "I'm a slow reader."

Reframe: "I currently read at 250 WPM. I am training to become a faster, more efficient reader. My speed is not my identity; it's a skill I'm developing."

Instead of: "I won't understand anything."

Reframe: "The science shows that focused, faster reading can improve comprehension. I am learning to trust my brain's ability to process meaning visually."

3. Developing Motivation and Consistency: The Engine of Progress

Motivation is what gets you started. Consistency is what gets you results. The key is to build systems that make consistency automatic, regardless of fleeting feelings of motivation.

Connect to Your Deeper "Why": Revisit the reasons from Chapter 1. Is it to get your degree faster? To advance your career? To finally read for pleasure? Write your top three reasons on a notecard and keep it with your practice materials. This is your emotional anchor.

Micro-Habits Over Grand Goals: "Practice speed reading for 20 minutes" can feel daunting. "Read one article with my pacer" is easy. Focus on the tiny, daily action. The grand goal will take care of itself. The chain of unbroken daily micro-habits is infinitely more powerful than sporadic bursts of effort.

Track and Celebrate: Use a calendar or habit tracker. Put a big, satisfying "X" on every day you complete your practice. This visual proof of progress is a powerful motivator in itself. Celebrate weekly improvements in your WPM, even if they are small.

Embrace the Dip: Every learning journey has a "dip"—a point where the initial excitement wears off and progress feels slow. This is normal. This is where most people quit. Understand that the dip is a sign that you are on the verge of a breakthrough. Perseverance through the dip is what separates successful learners from the rest.

4. *The Role of Positive Psychology in Learning*

Positive psychology is the scientific study of what makes life worth living. Its principles can be directly applied to skill acquisition to make the process more effective and fulfilling.

The Power of a Growth Mindset (Carol Dweck): This is the foundational belief that your abilities are not fixed traits but can be developed through dedication and hard work. Embrace challenges, persist in the face of setbacks, and see effort as the path to mastery. Every time you struggle with a technique, say, "My brain is growing right now."

Flow State: Speed reading, when you are fully immersed and focused, can induce a "flow state"—a condition of heightened focus and enjoyment. You can encourage flow by:

Clear Goals: "I will read this next page using only three fixations per line."

Immediate Feedback: Using your pacer and timer gives you instant feedback on your pace.

Balance of Challenge and Skill: The practice material should be slightly challenging but not overwhelming. This book is designed to provide this progressive challenge.

Savouring and Gratitude: At the end of each practice session, take 30 seconds to savour the accomplishment. Acknowledge the effort you put in. Feel a sense of gratitude for your brain's ability to learn and adapt. This positive reinforcement wires your brain to associate practice with reward, making you more likely to want to do it again.

Conclusion: The Prepared Mind

Technique is the "what" of speed reading. Mindset is the "how." By deliberately cultivating focus, dismantling limiting beliefs, building consistent habits, and applying the principles of positive psychology, you are doing more than just learning to read faster. You are training your mind to learn more effectively in any domain. You are building mental resilience. With this foundation firmly in place, you are now prepared to engage with the practical techniques not as a struggling novice, but as a confident learner ready to unlock your potential.

5

Exercises and Procedures: Building Your Speed Reading Muscle

Understanding the theory is the first step; now, it's time for practice. This chapter is your practical training manual. The exercises here are designed to systematically dismantle the inefficient habits covered in Chapter 2 and rebuild your reading process from the ground up. Like any form of training, consistency is more important than intensity. Diligent, daily practice of these drills, even for just 15-20 minutes, will yield remarkable results. Approach them with focus, patience, and a willingness to feel slightly uncomfortable—that feeling is your brain growing.

1. Warm-Up Drills for the Eyes

Just as a runner stretches before a sprint, your eyes need to warm up to perform at their peak. These drills improve ocular muscle control, reduce eye strain, and prepare your visual system for the rapid movements required in speed reading.

Exercise 1: Figure Eight

Procedure: Imagine a giant figure eight (the infinity symbol) on its side on a wall about 10 feet in front of you. Slowly trace the shape with your eyes, keeping your head perfectly still. Do this for 30 seconds clockwise, then 30 seconds counter-clockwise.

Purpose: Improves flexibility and control of your eye muscles, enhancing the smoothness of saccades.

Exercise 2: Near-Far Focus

Procedure: Hold your pen (your pacer) at arm's length, focusing on the tip. Then, slowly bring it towards the bridge of your nose, maintaining sharp focus. Stop when you can no longer keep it clear. Then, slowly push it back out. Repeat 10 times.

Purpose: Strengthens the ciliary muscles that control your lens, improving your ability to quickly adjust and maintain focus on the page, which reduces fatigue.

Exercise 3: Peripheral Awareness

Procedure: Hold your arms out to your sides and wiggle your fingers. Slowly bring your arms forward while staring straight ahead, using only your peripheral vision to detect the movement of your fingers. Stop when your fingers enter your central vision. Repeat 5 times.

Purpose: Actively engages and sensitizes your peripheral vision, a key component for expanding your perceptual span.

2. Word Grouping Exercises (Chunking)

The goal here is to break the word-by-word reading habit. You will train your eyes to see and your brain to process groups of words as a single unit of meaning.

Exercise 1: Two-Word Chunks

Procedure: Take a simple text. Using your pacer, draw two vertical slashes (||) between every two words. Your job is to read each pair of words in a single fixation.

Example: The || quick || brown || fox || jumps || over || the || lazy || dog.

Purpose: Forces your eyes to take in more than one word at a time, establishing the foundational rhythm of chunking.

Exercise 2: Phrasing

Procedure: Now, advance to grouping words into natural grammatical phrases. Use your pacer to underline these phrases. Read each underlined phrase in a single fixation.

Example: [The quick brown fox] [jumps over] [the lazy dog.]

Purpose: Teaches you to chunk not just random words, but meaningful units. This dramatically increases speed and comprehension, as you are processing ideas, not just vocabulary.

Exercise 3: Blanked Text

Procedure: Take a page of text and use a blank sheet of paper to cover everything except the line you are reading. As you move your pacer across the line, quickly pull the paper down to reveal the next line, and then cover the previous one. This prevents regression and forces forward momentum.

Purpose: Actively breaks the habit of skipping back, training your brain to trust its first processing of the text.

3. Peripheral Vision Expansion

This set of exercises is designed to widen your perceptual span, allowing you to see and comprehend words at the beginning and end of a line without directly fixating on them.

Exercise 1: Soft Focus

Procedure: Open a book to a page with a single column of text. Instead of focusing on the first word of a line, focus on the **white space in the center** of the line. Relax your eyes and try to perceive the words to the left and right of this central point without moving your eyes. The text will be blurry, but you should be able to recognize the shapes of the words.

Purpose: Trains your brain to rely on parafoveal and peripheral vision, reducing the number of fixations needed per line.

Exercise 2: Indentation Drill

Procedure: Using a ruler or two pacers, create a "visual margin." Place them vertically about 2-3 words in from the left margin and 2-3 words in from the right margin of the text. Your goal is to read the line by only making **one fixation** somewhere within this narrowed central column, using your peripheral vision to read the indented words.

Purpose: Physically demonstrates how much you can actually see in a single fixation, building confidence in your peripheral vision.

4. Timed Reading Drills

This is where you apply all the techniques under pressure to build raw speed. The goal here is pure velocity, pushing your brain to process text faster than it thinks it can.

The 3-2-1 Drill (The Core Speed Builder)

Round 1 (3 mins): Select a passage. Read for **3 minutes** using your pacer, pushing yourself to read as fast as you can while maintaining a bare minimum of comprehension. Mark your stopping point. Calculate your WPM.

Round 2 (2 mins): Immediately re-read the **same passage** from the beginning. You now have only 2 minutes to reach your previous stopping point. This forces your eyes and brain to recognize familiar chunks of text even faster.

Round 1 (1 min): For the final round, you have only **1 minute** to reach the same point. This feels impossible, but it successfully breaks your brain's self-imposed speed barrier.

Purpose: This is the most effective drill for overriding subvocalization and teaching your eyes to move at a new, faster rhythm.

5. Speed vs. Comprehension Tests

Speed is useless without understanding. These exercises ensure you are balancing both effectively and help you find your optimal reading pace.

Exercise 1: The Weekly Baseline Re-Test

Procedure: Once a week, exactly as you did in Chapter 2, conduct a formal test.

Select a **new, unfamiliar** passage of known word count.

Read it at your **top speed while aiming for full comprehension**. Time yourself and calculate your new WPM.

Immediately write down a summary of the passage or answer a set of pre-prepared questions. Rate your comprehension on a scale of 1-10 (10 being perfect recall).

Purpose: Provides objective, weekly data on your progress. The goal is a graph that shows both WPM and Comprehension scores rising together over time.

Exercise 2: The 60-Second Summary

Procedure: After any practice reading session (not a drill), set a timer for 60 seconds. Without looking back at the text, write or verbally articulate everything you can remember about what you just read. Focus on the main ideas, key arguments, and supporting evidence.

Purpose: Trains your brain to actively seek and retain meaning and structure while reading fast, not just to see words quickly. This transforms you from a passive receiver of information into an active engager with text.

Conclusion: The Cycle of Mastery

Your daily practice should be a cycle: Warm-Up -> Skill Drill (e.g., Chunking) -> Speed Drill (e.g., 3-2-1) -> Comprehension Check.

Do not be discouraged if comprehension dips temporarily during intense speed drills. This is normal. The weekly baseline test is your true measure of integrated progress. Trust the process. By systematically practicing these procedures, you are not just learning to read faster; you are fundamentally reprogramming your cognitive approach to the written word.

6

Preview & Scanning: Mastering the Pointer Technique

The single most immediate and impactful change you can make to your reading speed is to start using a pointer. This simple tool—a pen, your finger, or a digital stylus—is the catalyst that unlocks every other speed reading skill. It transforms reading from a passive, meandering activity into an active, disciplined process. This chapter is dedicated to mastering this fundamental technique. We will explore the science behind why it works so effectively, provide a step-by-step guide to its application, and outline progressive exercises to train your eye movements and systematically increase your pace from your baseline to remarkable new speeds.

1. Why Scanning with a Pointer Works: The Science of Guidance

Using a pointer is not a crutch; it is a precision tool that leverages your brain's innate wiring. Here's why it is non-negotiable for effective speed reading:

Eliminates Regression and Hesitation: The pointer moves forward relentlessly. This physical guide trains your brain to process information on the first pass, breaking the costly habit of unconsciously skipping back to re-read words. It instills rhythm and forward momentum.

Paces and Accelerates Your Eyes: Your eyes are naturally drawn to movement. The pointer acts as a metronome for your vision, setting a steady beat that you can gradually increase. Without a pacer, your eyes will naturally fall back into their old, slow rhythm of fixations and saccades.

Overrides Subvocalization: Your inner voice can only "speak" at about 250 WPM. By forcing your eyes to move faster than this rate, the pointer creates a physiological conflict that breaks the chain between seeing a word and "saying" it in your head. Your brain is forced to abandon the auditory pathway and rely on the faster visual processing centers.

Increases Concentration: The physical act of moving the pointer creates a kinesthetic connection to the task. It occupies a small part of your motor cortex, preventing your mind from wandering. It anchors your attention squarely on the text, dramatically reducing distractions and "third-world ruling."

2. How to Use a Pen or Pointer: Technique and Form

Proper technique is crucial. Using the pointer incorrectly can be just as inefficient as not using one at all.

Choosing Your Pointer: A fine-tipped pen or stylus is ideal. Its precise point allows for accurate guidance. Your finger can work but is broader and can obscure text.

The Grip: Hold the pointer in your dominant hand as if you were going to write with it, but rest the weight of your hand on the page or tablet. This prevents arm fatigue.

The Motion: Underlining, Not Highlighting:

Position: Place the tip of the pointer just **below** the line of text you are reading. Do not obscure the words.

Movement: Move the pointer smoothly and continuously along the line. The motion should come from your shoulder and wrist, not your fingers, for a fluid glide.

The Return: At the end of a line, quickly and smoothly zip the pointer back to the beginning of the next line. This "return sweep" should be as efficient as possible to minimize wasted time.

3. Eye Movement Training: Syncing Eye and Pointer

Your goal is to create a perfect partnership between the pointer and your eyes. The pointer leads; the eyes follow.

Exercise 1: The Follower Drill

Purpose: To break the habit of your eyes jumping ahead or lagging behind the pointer.

Procedure: Select a simple text. Focus 100% of your attention on the **tip of the pointer**. Your only job is to keep your eyes locked on that moving tip. Do not worry about comprehension. Simply practice moving your eyes in perfect sync with the pointer for one page. This feels unnatural at first but builds the essential neural connection.

Exercise 2: Perceptual Expansion Drill

Purpose: To train your peripheral vision to work with the pointer.

Procedure: As you move the pointer smoothly under the line, try to "soften" your focus. Instead of staring intensely at the point of the pointer, relax your gaze and be aware of the entire group of words immediately above it (3-4 words to the left and right). You are using the pointer as an anchor, but your peripheral vision is doing the bulk of the reading.

Exercise 3: Zig-Zag and Diagonal Sweeps (Advanced Scanning)

Purpose: For previewing text or reading very simple material, this technique allows for extremely rapid information gathering.

Procedure:

Zig-Zag: Move your pointer diagonally down the page in a gentle "S" or "Z" pattern, catching chunks of text at the beginning, middle, and end of each line.

Diagonal Sweep: Place your pointer at the top-left of a paragraph and sweep it diagonally down to the bottom-right in one smooth motion, allowing your peripheral vision to capture key words and ideas.

Note: These are **previewing and scanning techniques**, not methods for deep, analytical reading. They are used to get the gist of an article, find specific information, or identify a text's structure before a more detailed read.

4. Increasing Pace Gradually: The Metronome Method

The key to sustainable speed increase is gradual, consistent pressure. A sudden jump will cause comprehension to crash.

Step 1 - Establish Your Comfortable Pace: Use your pointer to read at a pace where comprehension feels easy and relaxed. This is your new baseline "guided" speed. It may already be faster than your old unguided speed.

Step 2 - The 5% Rule: Set a timer for 3 minutes. Read using your pointer. For the next 3-minute session, consciously push your pointer **just 5% faster**. The increase should feel slight but noticeable. Your brain will protest, and comprehension may feel strained. This is the point of growth.

Step 3 - Sustain and Stabilize: Read at this new, slightly faster pace for several sessions until it starts to feel more comfortable and comprehension stabilizes.

Step 4 - Repeat: Once the new pace feels natural, increase by another 5%. This iterative process of "push, stabilize, push again" is how you safely and effectively build speed without sacrificing understanding.

Utilize the 3-2-1 Drill: Revisit the 3-2-1 Drill from Chapter 5, but now perform it **exclusively with your pointer**. This drill is the ultimate application of paced, guided reading and will force massive speed breakthroughs.

Conclusion: The Foundation of All Advanced Techniques

The pointer technique is the bedrock of speed reading. Mastery of this single skill will yield greater immediate results than any other. It is the physical manifestation of the new, efficient reading habit you are building. Practice it diligently until the motion becomes second nature, until your eyes glide effortlessly alongside it, and until the rhythm of its movement dictates the new, faster rhythm of your thoughts. In the next chapter, we will build upon this foundation by teaching you how to preview and structure a text before you even begin to read, allowing you to harness this speed with powerful purpose and strategic understanding.

7

Scanning Using a Finger: Your Built-in Pacemaker

Think back to the very first time you learned to read. It's likely that a parent, teacher, or your own finger traced beneath the words, painstakingly moving from one symbol to the next. This was not a random act; it was a fundamental teaching tool. We are now, in a sense, returning to that foundational practice—not to learn what to read, but to rediscover how to read with unparalleled efficiency and focus.

In a world of digital distractions and information overload, the simple act of reading has become a fractured endeavor. Our eyes dart around the page, our minds wander, and we often find ourselves rereading the same sentence without comprehension. The solution to this modern malaise is astonishingly simple and profoundly effective: using your finger as a guide. This chapter is dedicated to transforming this elementary tool into your most powerful asset for cognitive enhancement. We will explore the multifaceted benefits of tactile guidance, master a repertoire of line-tracking methods suitable for any text, and engage in a comprehensive set of beginner-friendly exercises designed to rewire your reading habits from the ground up. Embracing this technique is the single greatest leap you can make toward becoming a consummate speed reader.

1. *The Profound Benefits of Tactile Guidance: The Neuroscience of Touch and Vision*

The effectiveness of the finger technique is not anecdotal; it is rooted in the principles of cognitive science and multi-sensory learning. Understanding the "why" behind the method will fuel your motivation to practice it consistently.

Engagement of the Kinesthetic Learning Pathway: A significant portion of the population are kinesthetic learners, meaning they process and retain information most effectively through physical activity and tactile engagement. By adding the physical dimension of moving your finger, you are no longer just a passive observer of text; you are an active participant in the process. This creates a powerful **multi-sensory feedback loop**: your eyes see the words, your brain decodes their meaning, and your finger physically feels the rhythm and pace of the narrative. This triple encoding of information dramatically enhances focus and makes the reading experience more immersive and memorable. It anchors your mind in the present moment, creating a bulwark against the incessant pull of distractions.

The Elimination of Intimidation and the Reduction of Anxiety: For many, the act of "studying" or "serious reading" is subconsciously associated with stress, pressure, and past difficulties. Picking up a highlighter or pen can trigger this anxiety. Your finger, however, is a neutral, innate part of you. It carries no baggage. Using it feels natural, casual, and low-pressure. This psychological shift is critical for beginners. It lowers the barrier to entry, making practice feel less like a chore and more like a discovery. This encourages daily consistency, which is the true engine of progress.

Unparalleled Availability and Versatility: The most sophisticated speed reading app is useless if you don't have your phone or tablet. A pen can be forgotten. Your finger, however, is a tool you always possess. This means you can practice and apply speed reading techniques in any scenario: poring over a complex textbook in the library, browsing a magazine in a doctor's office, reading a novel on the beach, or scrolling through an article on a touchscreen tablet. This constant availability ensures that every reading session becomes an opportunity for practice and improvement, seamlessly integrating your new skill into your daily life.

Promotion of "Soft Focus" and Peripheral Vision Expansion: The broad surface area of your fingertip, compared to the fine point of a pen, is a hidden advantage. It naturally encourages you to look at a **group of words** above the finger, rather than fixating on a single, specific point. This passively and intuitively trains your peripheral vision to expand and capture more text in a single glance. From the very first day, you are practicing chunking—the art of reading phrases instead of words—without even consciously trying.

The Dynamic Pacemaker Effect: Your finger acts as a physical metronome for your eyes. It sets a steady, controllable rhythm that dictates the pace of your reading. This is the most effective method for overcoming **subvocalization** (the inner voice that reads aloud in your head), which is limited to about 250 words per minute. By gradually increasing the speed of your finger's movement, you force your eyes and brain to keep up, pushing past this auditory bottleneck and training your visual cortex to process information at a much higher rate. The finger doesn't just guide; it pushes.

2. Mastering Line-Tracking Methods: A graduated Arsenal of Techniques

There is no single "right" way to use your finger. Different texts and different purposes call for different techniques. Master this graduated arsenal to become a versatile and adaptive reader.

Method 1: The Underliner – The Foundational Technique

Detailed Technique: Rest your hand comfortably on the page, wrist slightly elevated. Extend your index finger and place the **side**

of the fingertip (not the nail) just **below** the first word of the line. With a fluid, continuous motion originating from your shoulder and wrist—not your fingers—glide your finger in a straight line beneath the text from the left margin to the right. At the end of the line, perform a quick, efficient "return sweep," arcing your finger smoothly and swiftly back to the beginning of the next line. Minimize the time spent on this return motion.

Primary Application: This is the essential starting point for all beginners. It is ideal for dense, complex material like textbooks, legal documents, or technical manuals where high comprehension is paramount. It provides a clear, unwavering path that彻底消除回归（回读）。

Pro Tip: Imagine your finger is a train on a track. The track is straight and the train never reverses.

Method 2: The Tracer – For Enhanced Precision and Control

Detailed Technique: Once the Underliner method feels comfortable, advance to the Tracer. Here, you will place your fingertip **directly on** the page, tracing it along the **white space** immediately **below the baseline** of the words. The motion is more precise and requires finer motor control. The goal is to maintain a perfectly straight, smooth line through the center of the text.

Primary Application: This method is excellent for transitioning from physical books to digital screens, as it mimics the precision needed for touchscreen scrolling. It strengthens the connection between your focal point and the text, training your eyes for more advanced techniques.

Pro Tip: Practice on a sheet of lined paper first, tracing the line perfectly to build muscle memory for a straight trajectory.

Method 3: The Bouncer – Actively Training Chunking

Detailed Technique: This method actively breaks the habit of continuous, word-by-word reading. Instead of gliding, your finger will make two or three distinct, deliberate "bounces" or "hops" per line. For a standard line of text, you might bounce under the first meaningful phrase, the center of the line, and the last phrase. Your eyes will fixate on the point above each bounce, and your peripheral vision must capture the clusters of words in between.

Primary Application: Use this for reading newspapers, magazines, novels, and business reports—any material where you are reading for main ideas and narrative flow rather than intricate detail. This is the physical manifestation of phrase reading.

Pro Tip: Say the chunk of words in your mind as a single unit when you bounce. For example, for the phrase "the quick brown fox," think it as one idea, not four separate words.

Method 4: The Sweeper – The Art of Strategic Previewing

Detailed Technique: This is a specialized method for previewing a document or skimming for specific information. Use two or three fingers held together. Sweep them down the page in a gentle, fluid, "S"-shaped or zig-zag pattern. Your eyes are not reading every word; they are "surfing" the text, catching headings, bolded keywords, names, dates, and other salient features.

Primary Application: Use this before a deep read to create a mental map of the text's structure, main arguments, and key terms. It is also invaluable for researching online, reviewing meeting notes, or quickly determining if an article is relevant to your needs.

Pro Tip: Combine this with a specific goal: "I am sweeping this page to find the author's main conclusion" or "I need to find three supporting statistics."

3. A Comprehensive Regimen of Beginner-Friendly Exercises

Dedicate 15-20 minutes daily to this regimen. Consistency is vastly more important than duration.

Exercise 1: The Synchronization Drill (The "Blind" Read) - 5 Minutes

Primary Goal: To decouple the physical act of guiding from the cognitive act of comprehension, forging an automatic neural link between eye and finger.

Advanced Instructions: Select a book you are familiar with and turn it upside down. Use the Underliner method to guide your finger beneath the lines. Because the text is incomprehensible, your brain has no choice but to focus 100% of its attention on the task of synchronizing your eye movements with the movement of your finger. This intense, focused practice rapidly builds the muscle memory and neural pathways required for the technique to become automatic. After 2 minutes, turn the book right-side up and feel the dramatic improvement in the smoothness of your tracking.

Measure of Success: The movement feels fluid and effortless. Your eyes stay locked on your fingertip without consciously trying.

Exercise 2: The Pace Ladder Pyramid - 7 Minutes

Primary Goal: To systematically and safely expand your reading speed comfort zone by forcefully overriding subvocalization.

Advanced Instructions:

Base Rung (2 mins): Read a passage using your finger at a slow, comfortable, fully comprehensible pace. This is your baseline.

First Ascent (2 mins): Read the same passage again, but consciously move your finger 20-30% faster. Comprehension will feel strained. This is normal and desired. You are pushing past the speed of your inner voice.

The Peak (1 min): Read the same passage a third time, pushing for another 20-30% increase. Go faster than you think is possible. Do not worry about understanding; your goal is pure speed and rhythm.

Consolidation (2 mins): Immediately read a new passage at the speed you reached on the "First Ascent." Your brain, now acclimated to the faster "Peak" speed, will find this pace more manageable, and comprehension will partially rebound.

Measure of Success: The "First Ascent" speed begins to feel more natural and controllable within a few days of practice.

Exercise 3: The Dual-Task Comprehension Check-In - 5 Minutes

Primary Goal: To forcefully integrate speed with active comprehension and memory encoding.

Advanced Instructions: Read a new, short article (250-300 words) using your chosen finger method. As you read, hold a simple mental task in your mind: "What is the one central question this author is trying to answer?" or "What is the primary evidence used here?" When you finish, do not simply summarize. Instead, stand up and deliver a three-sentence "news report" out loud about what you just read, as if explaining it to someone else. The physical act of standing and speaking engages different neural networks, deeply cementing the information and proving to yourself that speed and understanding can coexist.

Measure of Success: You can confidently and concisely articulate the main idea and a key supporting point immediately after a speed read.

Conclusion: The Finger as Foundation

Mastering the finger technique is not the end of your journey; it is the solid foundation upon which all other advanced speed reading skills are built. It is the physical scaffold that supports the cognitive architecture of rapid information processing. By diligently practicing these methods and exercises, you are doing more than learning a trick; you are engaging in a form of cognitive training. You are teaching your brain to focus with laser-like intensity, to process visual information with unprecedented efficiency, and to navigate the vast seas of text with purpose, confidence, and exhilarating speed. Your finger is your guide, your pacemaker, and your key to unlocking a new world of reading potential

8

The Pinnacle of Skill: Mastering Eye-Only Scanning

Throughout this book, we have equipped you with powerful external aids: the pen, the finger, the pointer. These tools are the training wheels of speed reading—essential for building confidence, establishing rhythm, and breaking ingrained habits. But the ultimate objective is not to read faster with a crutch; it is to internalize these skills so completely that the crutch is no longer needed. This chapter marks your graduation to that highest level of proficiency: **Eye-Only Scanning**.

This is the art of guiding your eyes with the power of your mind alone. It is the seamless integration of all you have learned—chunking, reduced subvocalization, and expanded peripheral vision—into an invisible, internalized discipline. Here, your conscious mind is no longer focused on how to read; it is fully absorbed in what the text means. Mastering this skill transforms reading from a mechanical process into an intuitive and deeply efficient flow state. We will deconstruct the components of this ability, provide advanced exercises to expand your innate visual capacity, and introduce visualization methods that will allow you to project a "ghost pointer" onto the page, guiding your eyes with nothing but intention.

1. The Foundation of Eye-Only Scanning: From External to Internal Guidance

The transition from tool-assisted to tool-free reading is not about abandoning the techniques you've learned; it's about internalizing them. The rhythm, pace, and discipline imposed by your finger must now be generated by your cognitive command.

The Internal Metronome: Your first task is to develop an internal sense of pace. When using a pointer, your finger set the rhythm. Now, you must become the conductor of your own ocular orchestra. This begins with conscious control. Start by reading a line of text and mentally dictating the pace: "Go. Now. Now. Now." with each "Now" marking a intended fixation point. It will feel slow and forced at first, but this is the genesis of your internal pacemaker.

The "Ghost Pointer" Technique: As you read, visualize a point of light, a tiny arrow, or the tip of your finger moving beneath the line. Your eyes will have a natural tendency to follow this mental projection. This technique leverages **ideomotor phenomenon**—the influence of thought upon unconscious movement. By vividly imagining a guide, you can trigger the same smooth, left-to-right eye motion without any physical tool.

Maintaining Momentum and Preventing Regression: The greatest challenge of eye-only scanning is the temptation to revert to old habits—namely, regression (skip-backs). Without the physical barrier of a pointer moving relentlessly forward, your eyes might wander. To combat this, you must cultivate a mindset of **forward trust.** You must trust your brain to process the information on the first pass. When you feel the urge to jump back, consciously override it with a forceful mental command: "Keep moving forward." This mental discipline is the final barrier to full autonomy.

2. Expanding Your Fixation Span: The Key to True Speed

The single most important factor in tool-free speed reading is the number of words you can capture in a single fixation. A narrow span means more fixations per line, which means slower reading. A wide span means fewer fixations, which means faster reading. This is the mathematical heart of speed reading.

Understanding the Visual Field:

Foveal Vision: The central 2-3 degrees of your vision. This is your high-resolution, sharp focus area, perfect for recognizing detail (like a single word).

Parafoveal Vision: The area extending out to about 5-6 degrees on either side of the fovea. This vision is less sharp but can recognize word shapes and lengths.

Peripheral Vision: Everything beyond that, which detects motion and gross shapes.

The Goal: To train your parafoveal vision to do more of the work. You want to fixate your fovea on a central word in a line and use your parafoveal vision to clearly recognize the words on either side, effectively reading 3-5 words in a single glance.

Advanced Exercise 1: The Central Fixation Drill

Purpose: To break the habit of looking at the first word of a line and force your parafoveal vision into action.

Procedure: Take a page of text with a single column. Instead of placing your first fixation on the first word of a line, force yourself to fixate on the **second or even third word**. Use your peripheral vision to perceive the first word(s) to the left. As you finish the line, your last fixation should be on the second or third word from the end, perceiving the final words with your left peripheral vision.

Why it Works: This is an uncomfortable but immensely powerful drill. It physically demonstrates that you don't need to look directly at a word to recognize it. It stretches your perceptual span beyond its comfort zone.

Advanced Exercise 2: The Pyramidal Reading Drill

Purpose: To systematically widen the number of words you process per fixation.

Procedure:

Level 1: Read a paragraph, consciously aiming to see **two words** in every fixation. Use the "bounce" rhythm from the finger method, but now just with your eyes.

Level 2: Read the same paragraph again, now aiming for three words per fixation. You will need to find a new, slower rhythm and softer focus.

Level 3: Attempt to read the same paragraph with only **two fixations per line**. This will feel impossible at first. Your eyes will want to grab the beginning, middle, and end of the line in three rapid fixations.

Why it Works: This progressive overload for your eye muscles and visual processing system forces a permanent expansion of your capabilities.

Advanced Exercise 3: The Soft Focus / Wide Angle Drill

Purpose: To shift from intense, narrow focus to a relaxed, wide-angle awareness of the text.

Procedure: Open a book to a page. Instead of "looking at" the words, relax your eyes and try to be aware of the entire page at once. Let the text appear slightly blurry. Now, without moving your eyes from the center of the page, try to perceive the white space in the margins, the shape of the paragraphs, and the overall structure. Then, as you begin to read a line, maintain this softer, wider awareness. Don't "stare" at the words; "absorb" them from within this wider field of view.

Why it Works: This counter-intuitive exercise breaks the habit of "tunnel vision" reading. The strain of intense focus actually reduces your field of view. Relaxing your eyes allows your natural peripheral vision to expand to its full potential.

3. Visualization Methods: The Mind's Guide

When the physical tool is gone, visualization becomes your most powerful asset. These methods use the power of your imagination to structure the text and guide your eyes.

Method 1: The Chunking Highlighter

Technique: As you approach a line of text, before you even begin to read it, quickly **visualize** it being already highlighted in meaningful chunks of 3-4 words. See a soft, yellow highlight over "the quick brown fox" and another over "jumps over the" and a final one over "lazy dog." Your eyes will then naturally jump to the beginning of each highlighted section, processing the chunks as single units.

Application: This is exceptionally useful for dense prose where meaning is grouped in phrases. It forces you to perform syntactic analysis at a glance, improving both speed and comprehension.

Method 2: The Z-Pattern Sweep

Technique: For previewing a page or reading lighter text, visualize a faint, glowing "Z" or zig-zag pattern superimposed over the text. Your eyes will follow this imaginary pattern, sweeping from the top-left to top-right, diagonally down to the left of the next line, and then across to the right again. This allows you to cover a page in seconds, catching nouns, verbs, and headings to build a rapid mental scaffold of the content.

Application: Perfect for reviewing reports, articles, or chapters you've already read, or for quickly assessing the relevance of new material.

Method 3: The Central Vertical Line

Technique: Imagine a faint, vertical line running down the center of the text column. Now, instead of reading left to right, your goal is to simply **float your eyes down this central line.** You are not trying to read individual words sequentially. You are allowing the words on both sides of the line to flow into your parafoveal and peripheral vision. Your brain will automatically stitch this information together.

Application: This is an advanced, high-speed technique for very familiar material or for final reviews of text you have already studied. It feels less like reading and more like absorbing the essence of the page.

The Integrated Practice Routine for Mastery

Dedicate time to this sequential routine to internalize these skills:

Warm-Up (2 mins): Use the Soft Focus Drill on a page of text to relax your eyes and expand your awareness.

Skill Drill (5 mins): Practice the **Central Fixation Drill** on a new paragraph, consciously starting and ending each line 2-3 words in from the margins.

Speed Drill (5 mins): Perform a **Pace Ladder** drill (see Chapter 5) but now **using only the "Ghost Pointer"** technique to guide your eyes. Push your speed in each round.

Comprehension Integration (3 mins): Read a final paragraph using the **Chunking Highlighter** visualization. Then, close the book and write a one-sentence summary of every two paragraphs you read.

Conclusion: The Silent Symphony of Reading

Mastering eye-only scanning is the final piece of the puzzle. It represents the full integration of the physical, the visual, and the cognitive into a silent, effortless symphony of understanding. The page is no longer a sequence of words to be laboriously decoded but a field of meaning to be absorbed. The frantic, jerky eye movements of the past are replaced by a smooth, rhythmic, and purposeful flow. You are no longer a reader struggling with a text; you are a mind engaging with ideas, unencumbered by the mechanics of the process. This is the freedom and the power that the skills in this book have been designed to unlock. It is the art of reading, perfected.

9

The Quantum Leap: Reading Phrases Rather Than Words

The Unit of Thought

Consider the following sentence: "The old man walked his dog in the park every evening."

A slow, word-by-word reader processes this as seven separate units of data:

The -> old -> man -> walked -> his -> dog -> in -> the -> park -> every -> evening.

Their conscious mind must then assemble these pieces like a puzzle to extract the meaning: an elderly gentleman routinely took his canine companion for a stroll in a public garden at dusk.

A phrase reader, however, sees not eleven words, but three or four meaningful chunks:

[The old man] [walked his dog] [in the park] [every evening].

Their brain receives pre-assembled ideas. The cognitive load is drastically reduced, speed is dramatically increased, and because the brain is receiving information in logical packets, comprehension and retention are often improved.

This chapter is dedicated to making this fundamental shift. We will move from reading lexically (word-for-word) to reading ideationally (idea-by-idea). This is not a minor adjustment; it is a quantum leap in reading efficiency. We will explore the cognitive science behind chunking, train your brain to recognize linguistic patterns instantly, and provide a rigorous set of exercises to rewire your reading process from the ground up. Mastering this skill is the most significant thing you can do to permanently and sustainably increase your reading speed.

1. *Chunking Words into Meaningful Phrases: The Architecture of Language*

Chunking, in a reading context, is the cognitive process of grouping individual pieces of information—letters into words, words into phrases—into larger, more manageable units. It is how the brain manages the limitations of working memory.

The Cognitive Science: Miller's Magic Number 7 (±2)
Psychologist George Miller's famous research found that the average human's working memory can hold only about 7 ± 2 items at once. When you read word-by-word, you are filling these precious slots with individual words (the, old, man, walked, his, dog…). You reach capacity quickly, forcing your brain to dump early words to make room for new ones, leading to poor comprehension and the need to regress.

However, a "chunk" can be a single item that contains multiple pieces of information. The phrase [The old man] is one chunk containing three words. By chunking, you effectively expand the capacity of your working memory from 7 words to 7 ideas, each of which may contain 3-5 words. This is how you can read faster and remember more simultaneously.

How to Identify a Phrase:
A meaningful phrase is not a random group of words. It is a grammatical unit that acts as a single part of speech. Train your eyes to look for these natural groupings:

Noun Phrases: The subject or object of the sentence. (The quick brown fox, a devastatingly beautiful painting, the theory of relativity).

Verb Phrases: The action of the sentence. (will have been sleeping, ran quickly down the street, is a renowned scientist).

Prepositional Phrases: Phrases that show relationship, usually about time or place. (in the house, after the devastating storm, with great enthusiasm).

Clauses: Groups of words containing a subject and a verb (because the weather was nice, who lives next door).

2. Pattern Recognition in Sentences: Seeing the Matrix

The English language, for all its complexity, is built on predictable patterns. Your brain is already a supercomputer for recognizing these patterns in speech; we must now apply this ability to reading.

The S-V-O Pattern: The most common sentence structure in English is Subject-Verb-Object.

[The investor] (S) [sold] (V) [her shares] (O).

[The committee] (S) [will announce] (V) [its decision] (O) [tomorrow] (modifier).

Your brain can be trained to instantly lock onto this structure. Find the subject (who/what is this about?), then the verb (what are they doing?), then the object (to whom/what are they doing it?). The rest of the words simply modify these core components.

Signal Words and Punctuation: These are the signposts that define the boundaries of chunks.

Articles & Determiners (a, an, the, my, some) often signal the start of a noun phrase.

Prepositions (in, on, at, by, with) almost always signal the start of a prepositional phrase.

Conjunctions (and, but, or, because) often signal the start of a new clause or idea.

Commas, semicolons, and periods are clear visual markers for the end of a chunk or a complete thought.

The Role of Peripheral Vision: This is where the physical act meets the cognitive. As your fixation point lands on the center of a phrase, your parafoveal vision (the area just outside direct focus) must be trained to take in the entire chunk. You are not reading sequentially within the chunk; you are absorbing it as a single, recognizable image or unit of meaning. This is why the finger exercises were so important—they trained your eyes to take in a wider field of view.

3. A Progressive Exercise Regimen for Phrase Reading

This is a practical, step-by-step training program. Dedicate 15-20 minutes daily to these exercises.

Exercise 1: Pre-Chunked Reading (The Guided Tour) - 5 Minutes

Goal: To teach your eyes and brain what phrases look and feel like.

Materials: Use a book you don't mind marking up, or print articles from the internet.

Procedure: Take a paragraph and, using a pencil, draw vertical lines | between natural | phrases | like this |. Your job is to read each grouped phrase in a single fixation. Use your finger or a pen to pace yourself, placing one fixation (one "look") on each chunk. Do not read the words individually; try to "photograph" the entire chunk and absorb its meaning as a whole.

Progression: Start with 2-3 word chunks. As you improve, create larger chunks, grouping short prepositional phrases with their connected nouns or verbs (e.g., [walked his dog] [in the park]).

Exercise 2: The Phrase Flash Drill - 5 Minutes

Goal: To develop instant recognition of phrase units, eliminating subvocalization.

Materials: Index cards or a presentation app on your device (like PowerPoint).

Procedure: Write or type a single meaningful phrase on each card/slide (e.g., "The global economy," "is experiencing significant volatility," "due to recent geopolitical events."). Flash each card for a fraction of a second (start with 0.5 seconds and reduce time as you improve). Your goal is not to "read" the words but to recognize the meaning of the entire phrase instantly. This drill is too fast for subvocalization to occur, forcing your brain into a direct visual-to-meaning processing mode.

Exercise 3: Rhythm and Pacing with a Metronome - 5 Minutes

Goal: To internalize the rhythm of phrase reading.

Materials: A metronome app (set to beat per minute) and a text.

Procedure: Set the metronome to a slow pace (e.g., 40 BPM). On each beat, your eyes should move to a new fixation point and take in a new phrase. [Beat 1: The old man] [Beat 2: walked his dog] [Beat 3: in the park] [Beat 4: every evening]. As this becomes easy, gradually increase the tempo of the metronome. This trains your brain to process phrases at a faster and faster rhythm, systematically increasing your words-per-minute rate.

Exercise 4: The "Thought-Unit" Summary - 5 Minutes

Goal: To cement the connection between phrase reading and enhanced comprehension.

Procedure: Read a page of new material using your phrase reading technique. Instead of summarizing the page by what you remember, summarize it by the **number of key ideas or chunks** you extracted.

Example: "This page had about four main ideas: [1] the definition of chunking, [2] Miller's magic number theory, [3] the types of phrases, and [4] the first exercise."

Why it Works: This post-reading analysis shifts your focus from recalling words to recalling concepts. It proves to you that you are reading for meaning, not just speed, and that the two are synergistic.

Conclusion: From Decoding to Absorbing

Moving from words to phrases is the transition from being a mechanic who examines every single part of an engine to being a driver who simply turns the key and goes. You are shifting your cognitive effort from the exhausting low-level process of decoding symbols to the high-level, engaging process of absorbing ideas, evaluating arguments, and making connections.

This skill does not develop overnight. It requires consistent practice to rewire a lifetime of word-by-word reading. There will be frustration. You will sometimes feel your comprehension dip before it soars. But if you persist with these exercises, you will cross a threshold. The choppy stream of individual words will smooth into a flowing river of ideas. You will no longer see text; you will see thought. And in that space, true reading mastery is found.

10

The Frontier of Performance: Advanced Speed Reading Techniques

❧

Transcending the Fundamentals

You have built a formidable foundation. You have mastered the use of a pacer, tamed subvocalization, expanded your peripheral vision, and learned to read in meaningful phrases. You are no longer a passive decoder of text but an active conductor of the reading process. Now, we venture into the frontier. This chapter is dedicated to the techniques that separate the proficient from the elite—the methods that will allow you to push your reading speed to its biological and cognitive limits.

These are not mere "tips and tricks." They are sophisticated, integrated practices that require a deep understanding of the principles covered in previous chapters. They demand intense focus, disciplined practice, and a willingness to temporarily sacrifice comprehension for the sake of breaking through speed barriers. We will explore the art of **Meta-Guiding**, the strategy of **Reading in Blocks**, the final assault on **Subvocalization**, and the pinnacle of visual processing: **Multiple-Line Scanning**. Approach these techniques as a master craftsman would approach a new set of precision tools—with respect, patience, and the intent to master them completely.

1. Meta-Guiding: Forcing the Eye to Obey

Meta-guiding is the advanced evolution of using a pointer. While a finger or pen provides a physical guide, meta-guiding is the conscious, willful command of your eye's fixation points. You are not just following a path; you are dictating it with precision.

The Concept: The term "meta" means "beyond" or "higher." Meta-guiding is the higher-order function of guiding your cognitive process by controlling your visual input. It is the deliberate placement of your eye's focus on specific, pre-determined points in the text to maximize information intake per unit of time.

The Technique:

Pre-Scan: Before reading a line, your peripheral vision should perform a micro-scan to identify the natural chunks within it (e.g., a noun phrase at the start, a verb phrase in the middle).

Command the Fixation: Instead of letting your eyes drift, you consciously choose where to look. You command your eyes to fixate on the center of the most information-dense chunk. For the line [The financial report] [indicates a significant] [quarterly profit increase], you would place three fixations: one in the center of each bracketed phrase.

Control the Duration: Advanced meta-guiding involves not just where you look, but for how long. For familiar concepts or simple connectors (e.g., "and," "the," "of"), your fixation should be a mere flicker—a few milliseconds. For complex, novel, or critical terms, you allow a slightly longer pause to fully download the meaning.

Training Drill: The Dot Drill

Procedure: Take a page of text and, with a pencil, place a small, faint dot at the intended center of each phrase you want to read. Your sole task is to move your eyes rapidly from dot to dot, absorbing the meaning of the entire phrase from that single fixation point. This drill trains your brain to trust the information gathered from a precisely targeted glance.

2. *Reading in Blocks: The Paragraph as a Unit*

Reading in phrases is a massive leap. Reading in blocks is the next evolutionary step. This technique involves processing large segments of text—often an entire sentence or a full clause—in one or two fixations.

The Concept: The goal is to perceive the shape and structure of a paragraph visually, almost as an image, and to extract its core meaning without sequentially processing every line. You are moving from reading sentences to reading ideas.

The Technique:

Soft Focus: Relax your eyes and allow your vision to de-focus slightly. You are not looking at the words; you are looking through the text at the paragraph as a whole.

Identify Anchors: Let your eyes be drawn to the key elements that stand out: **nouns, verbs, and** numbers. Your brain is an expert pattern-recognition machine. It will automatically latch onto the words that carry the most meaning: "CEO," "announced," "merger," "$5 billion."

Trust Your Brain: Your cognitive faculties will use these anchors to infer the relationships and fill in the gaps using context and grammatical expectation. You are not reading every word; you are allowing the meaning to emerge from the pattern.

Training Drill: The 3-Second Gist

Procedure: Open a book to a new page. Give yourself only **3 seconds** to look at a paragraph. Then, immediately look away and write down or state aloud the core idea of that paragraph. What is it about? What is the key action or argument? You will be wrong often at first, but this drill forces your brain to abandon detail-oriented reading and switch to holistic meaning extraction.

3. The Final Barrier: Eliminating Subvocalization

While we have managed to reduce subvocalization, for true elite speeds, it must be eliminated for vast portions of text. This is not about suppressing your inner voice; it's about switching to a purer, faster mode of thought.

The Concept: Subvocalization is the auditory processing of text. The goal is to transition to **visual ideation**—processing the meaning of words and phrases directly as concepts, images, and feelings, without the intermediate, slow step of "hearing" them in your mind.

Advanced Techniques:

Number and Symbol Recognition: Your brain doesn't subvocalize the meaning of "@" or "&" or "100." You understand them visually. Train yourself to see words as visual symbols in the same way. See the word "dog" not as a sound to be heard, but as a symbol that directly triggers the concept of a furry, four-legged animal.

Pacing Beyond the Auditory Threshold: This is the most effective method. Use your pacer to move at a speed so fast that it is literally impossible for your inner voice to keep up. If your inner voice maxes out at 250 WPM, force your eyes to move at 400, then 500 WPM. Your inner voice will stutter, then fall silent, and your brain will have no choice but to rely on the visual processing centers to grab the meaning. It will be chaotic and comprehension will drop initially, but this is the necessary "breakthrough" phase.

Chew Gum or Hum: This is a classic and highly effective psychomotor trick. By engaging the muscles used for speech (jaw, tongue, diaphragm) in an unrelated activity like chewing gum or humming a tune, you create neural interference. You physically inhibit the subtle motor signals that trigger subvocalization, preventing it from occurring.

Training Drill: The Speed Blur

Procedure: Select a relatively easy text. Using your finger or a pen, guide your eyes down the page at an extremely fast, constant speed—a speed so fast that you cannot possibly comprehend everything. Your goal is not to understand, but to **see**. Let the words blur together. Practice this for one minute, then stop. You will likely have a vague, impressionistic sense of the topic. This drill's purpose is purely physiological: to break the chain between eye movement and auditory processing.

4. Multiple-Line Scanning: The Pinnacle of Speed

This is the ultimate application of expanded peripheral vision and soft focus. Multiple-line scanning is the ability to process two, three, or even more lines of text in a single fixation.

The Concept: Instead of moving your eyes left-to-right, you move them down the page in a steady, vertical flow. Your wide perceptual span allows you to read the entire width of the column from a single point of focus.

The Technique:

The Vertical Guide: Use your pacer to draw a straight, smooth line down the **center** of the text column.

The "Z" Pattern: For wider text, use a gentle, shallow "Z" or zig-zag pattern. Your eyes sweep from the top-left of the paragraph, diagonally down to the bottom-right, capturing the lines in between with your peripheral vision.

The S-Sweep: A more advanced pattern involves moving your eyes in a soft "S" shape down the page, allowing you to catch the beginning and end of each line in your central vision as you curve through the column.

Training Drill: The Newspaper Column Drill

Procedure: This technique is ideally practiced on text arranged in a single, narrow column (like a newspaper or a PDF with a two-column layout). Use a ruler or a blank piece of paper to cover all but a 2-3 inch wide column of text. Now, practice pulling your pacer straight down the center of this column at a steady pace. Your goal is to absorb the meaning from the entire width of the narrow column without moving your eyes horizontally. This is the perfect environment to train your eyes and brain for this demanding skill.

Integrating Advanced Techniques: A Sample Routine

Do not attempt all of this at once. Integrate one technique at a time into your practice.

Warm-up (2 mins): Vertical Guide Drill on a narrow column.

Skill Focus (10 mins): Dedicate this time to one technique only. E.g., Monday: Meta-Guiding with the Dot Drill. Tuesday: Reading in Blocks with the 3-Second Gist. Wednesday: Pacing Beyond Auditory Threshold.

Comprehension Integration (5 mins): Read a full page using your new skill, but at a slightly reduced pace that allows for ~70% comprehension. Write a brief summary.

Cool-down (3 mins): Re-read the same page at a normal, comfortable pace to catch any nuances you missed.

Conclusion: The Art and Science of Mastery

These advanced techniques are the tools of a master. They require not just physical eye control, but a profound trust in your brain's ability to synthesize meaning from patterns. There will be days of frustration where comprehension seems to vanish. This is not failure; it is the necessary process of cognitive rewiring. You are building new neural highways, and construction is always messy.

Persist. The payoff is a reading experience that is fundamentally different from what you once knew. Text becomes a fluid medium you swim through, not a wall you decipher. You gain the ability to modulate your speed based on your purpose—from a slow, careful crawl for a complex contract to a breathtaking sprint through a novel. This is the final step in claiming true sovereignty over the written word.

11

The Point of No Return: Eliminating Regression and Training Forward-Only Reading

The Tyranny of the Backwards Glance

Imagine driving a car while constantly tapping the brakes and frequently looking in the rearview mirror. Your progress would be slow, jerky, and unsafe. This is precisely what you are doing when you allow yourself to regress—to skip back and re-read text you have already passed.

Regression is the arch-nemesis of speed reading. It is a silent thief of time and a major disruptor of comprehension. Studies suggest that the average reader can spend up to 30% of their total reading time unconsciously re-reading material. This chapter is a dedicated assault on this costly habit. We will delve into the psychological roots of regression, master the mindset of forward momentum, and employ powerful physical and cognitive exercises—using simple covering tools—to permanently break the cycle of looking back. Mastering this single skill will provide one of the most immediate and dramatic boosts to your reading efficiency.

1. The Why Behind the Glance: Understanding and Preventing Regression

To eliminate a habit, we must first understand its causes. Regression is rarely a conscious choice; it is typically an unconscious response to one of several underlying triggers:

Lack of Confidence (The Chief Culprit): The most common cause is a simple lack of trust in your own brain's ability to comprehend information on the first pass. A moment of doubt arises—"Did I get that?"—and the eyes instantly jump back to seek reassurance, creating a self-fulfilling prophecy of inefficiency.

Poor Concentration ("Third World Ruling"): When your mind wanders due to external distractions or internal monologue, your eyes continue moving across the page. When you "snap back" to the text, you find yourself in a new location with no memory of how you got there, forcing a regression to your last conscious point.

Unfamiliar Vocabulary or Complex Concepts: Encountering a difficult word or a dense sentence can cause a mental "stutter." Instead of processing it in context or moving on temporarily, the instinct is to stop and re-read the challenging section, often multiple times.

Perfectionism: Some readers hold the false belief that they must understand and retain every single word with 100% clarity. This unrealistic standard creates anxiety and a compulsive need to re-read to achieve an impossible perfection.

Poor Eye Movement Control: Without the guide of a pacer, eyes can naturally make erratic movements, sometimes slipping back to a previous line unintentionally.

The Psychological Shift: Cultivating Forward Trust
The solution begins in the mind. You must adopt a new mantra: **"Forward Momentum Yields Better Comprehension."**
Understand that:

Context is King: Often, the meaning of a slightly missed word or a confusing phrase becomes clear from the context of the following sentences. Regression robs you of this clarifying context.

The Brain is a Predictor: Your brain is not a passive receiver of information; it is an active predictor. It constantly anticipates what comes next based on what it has already processed. Regression disrupts this predictive flow and actually lowers overall comprehension.

The Goal is Ideas, Not Words: You are reading for the author's central thesis and supporting arguments, not for photographic recall of every adjective. Trust that you are capturing the essential meaning on the first pass.

2. Training Forward-Only Reading: The Mechanics of Momentum

This is a active skill that must be trained. It involves both a physical technique and a mental discipline.

The Role of the Pacer (Revisited): Your finger or pen is your first and most important defense against regression. Its relentless forward movement provides a physical barrier and a psychological command: "Do not go back." The constant motion keeps you anchored in the present moment of the text.

The "Read It and Leave It" Mindset: Approach each line, each chunk, and each phrase as a discrete unit. Once your pacer has passed over it, consider it processed. It is filed away. Your focus must immediately and entirely shift to the next unit of text. There is no going back to the "file cabinet"; you keep moving forward to build the complete picture.

The "Note-to-Self" Technique: If you encounter a truly confusing concept or an unfamiliar term that you know is critical, do not regress. Instead, make a **small, light pencil mark** in the margin next to the line or make a quick mental note. Promise yourself that you will return to it after you have finished the section or chapter. Ninety percent of the time, the concept will be clarified by the subsequent text, making the return trip unnecessary. This strategy acknowledges the concern without sacrificing forward momentum.

3. Exercises with Covering Tools: Forcing the Habit of Forward Motion

The most effective way to break the regression habit is to make it physically impossible. These exercises use simple tools to aggressively train your eyes and brain to move forward.

Exercise 1: The Blank Sheet Method (The Ultimate Trainer)

Tools: One blank sheet of paper or an index card.

Procedure: Place the blank sheet above the line you are currently reading. As you read each line, **pull the sheet down to cover it immediately.** The text you have just read disappears from view. It is gone. You cannot go back even if you want to. This is the most powerful exercise for eliminating regression because it removes all choice.

Progression:

Level 1: Cover each line after you read it. This breaks the habit of intra-line regression (jumping back within a sentence).

Level 2: Cover each paragraph after you read it. This breaks the habit of inter-line regression (jumping back to previous sentences or lines).

Level 3: Cover each page after you read it. This trains you for long-term retention and trust in your comprehension over larger stretches of text.

Exercise 2: The Downward Slider

Tools: A ruler or a business card.

Procedure: Place the ruler horizontally underneath the line you are reading. This highlights your current line and obscures the lines below, reducing visual clutter. As you finish each line, **slide the ruler down** to reveal the next line and cover the one you just read. The constant downward motion reinforces forward momentum and provides a clear visual focus for your eyes.

Exercise 3: The Pace-Ladder Under Pressure

Tools: Your pacer and a timer.

Procedure: Revisit the 3-2-1 Drill from Chapter 5, but with a new, strict rule: **Regression is an absolute failure.** If you catch your eyes jumping back, you must restart the timer. The intense time pressure of this drill, combined with the zero-tolerance rule for regression, forces your brain to find new strategies for comprehension on the fly. It learns that skipping back is not an option, so it must become more efficient on the first pass.

Exercise 4: The Comprehension Confidence Builder

Tools: A book and a voice recorder or a study partner.

Procedure: Select a short article or a book chapter. Read it from start to finish using the Blank Sheet Method to absolutely prevent any regression. When you are done, **immediately close the book** and record a verbal summary of everything you remember for one minute. Alternatively, explain it to your study partner.

Analysis: You will almost certainly be surprised by how much you retained. This exercise provides tangible, undeniable proof that your brain is capable of high comprehension without regression. This evidence is the strongest weapon you have against the doubt that causes the habit in the first place.

Integrating the "No Regression" Rule into Daily Reading

The goal is to make forward-only reading your default mode.

Awareness: The first step is simply to notice when you do it. For one day, read without trying to change anything. Just be aware of every single time your eyes jump backwards. Acknowledge it without judgment.

Tool-Based Practice: Spend one week doing 15 minutes of daily practice using the **Blank Sheet Method**. Be ruthless. This will feel frustrating but is necessary to break the neural pathway.

Application: After a week of dedicated practice, begin your normal reading sessions with your pacer and a conscious vow not to regress. When you feel the urge, remember the feeling of the blank sheet covering the text and use your "Note-to-Self" technique instead.

Progressive Difficulty: Start with easy, engaging material (like a novel or news magazine) before applying the rule to dense textbooks or technical manuals.

Conclusion: Unshackling Your Potential

Eliminating regression is one of the most liberating steps in your speed reading journey. It unshackles you from the past and unleashes you into a fluid, forward-moving reading experience. The constant, nagging doubt is replaced by a confident flow. The time you once wasted on backward glances is now redeemed, compounding into hours of saved time over weeks and months of reading.

By using these covering tools and mental disciplines, you are not just learning a technique; you are fundamentally rewiring your relationship with text. You are building an unshakable trust in your own cognitive abilities. You are learning to read with the confident momentum of a river flowing to the sea—always moving forward, never looking back.

ⵊⵊⵊ

12

The Strategic Art of Sliding and Skimming: Reading with Purpose

The Misunderstood Power of Skimming

Skimming is often mistakenly viewed as a "cheat" or a form of "half-reading"—a lazy shortcut that sacrifices depth for speed. This is a profound misconception. In the toolkit of an advanced reader, **skimming is not a substitute for reading; it is a specific, powerful mode of reading with a unique purpose.** It is the strategic art of extracting the maximum amount of core information with the minimum investment of time and cognitive resources. It is the radar sweep that identifies the target before the laser focus is applied.

This chapter will redefine skimming as a critical and sophisticated skill. We will move beyond the simplistic idea of "just looking for the important bits" and provide a precise, actionable system for how to slide through text with intention. You will learn how to differentiate between structural signposts and filler words, how to tailor your approach based on your specific goal, and how to integrate skimming into a broader reading strategy for both study and leisure. Mastering this skill will make you an incredibly efficient information processor, capable of triaging content, prioritizing your attention, and conquering vast volumes of text with strategic precision.

1. *Skimming for Key Ideas: The Architecture of Information*

Effective skimming is not random. It is a systematic process of hunting for the architectural elements that give a text its structure and meaning. Your goal is to construct a mental skeleton of the content.

The Pre-Read: The 60-Second Map
Before you read a single word for depth, spend 60 seconds skimming the entire piece to answer these questions:

What is the overall structure? (e.g., Introduction -> Three Arguments -> Case Study -> Conclusion)

What is the main thesis? (Usually found in the abstract, introduction, or conclusion).

What are the major supporting points? (Often revealed by headings and topic sentences).

This pre-read creates a "mental map." When you then read in detail, you are no longer navigating a dark, unknown forest; you are following a well-marked trail, which dramatically improves retention and speed.

The Skimmer's Hit List: What to Look For
Train your eyes to be drawn like a magnet to these high-value elements:

Headings and Subheadings: These are the chapter titles and section headers of the author's argument. They provide the highest-level outline.

Introduction and Conclusion Paragraphs: The introduction usually states the purpose and main point. The conclusion summarizes the key findings and arguments. Reading these two sections alone can often give you 80% of the core idea.

Topic Sentences (The First Sentence of a Paragraph): In well-structured writing, the first sentence of a paragraph introduces the main idea of that paragraph. The subsequent sentences provide evidence, examples, and explanation. Skimming the first sentence of every paragraph builds a coherent summary of the entire argument.

Visual Cues: Bold, italicized, and <u>underlined</u> text, as well as **bullet points** and numbered lists, are all flags planted by the author saying, "This is important!"

Names, Dates, and Numbers: These concrete details often signify key evidence, statistics, or references, making them prime targets for a skimmer.

Transition Words and Phrases: Words like "Therefore," "However," "Consequently," "For example," and "In contrast" signal a shift in logic, the introduction of evidence, or a counter-argument. They tell you how the ideas connect.

2. Spotting Important vs. Filler Words: The Signal and the Noise

The English language is filled with redundancy. A huge percentage of words in any given text are structural filler, not core meaning. A skilled skimmer learns to see through the noise to find the signal.

The "Filler" Categories (The Noise):

Function Words: These are the grammatical glue: the, a, an, of, for, by, in, on, at, to, is, are, was, were, be, being, been. While essential for grammar, they carry little meaning on their own.

Excessive Adjectives and Adverbs: Words like very, really, quite, extremely, incredibly, beautiful, quickly often add flavor but not fundamental substance. The core noun and verb are more important.

Common Verbs: Have, do, get, make, go are often used in generic ways.

Polite Formulations and Hedging: Phrases like "It is important to note that," "One could argue that," "In my opinion," often preface the actual point and can be skipped over.

The "Important" Categories (The Signal):

Nouns: Especially **proper nouns** (names, places) and **concrete nouns** (e.g., computer, treaty, engine, molecule). These are the "what."

Power Verbs: These are the specific, action-oriented words that drive meaning: accelerate, synthesize, dismantle, advocate, collapse, generate. These are the "what happened."

Unique Adjectives and Adverbs: While many are filler, those that change meaning significantly are key: flawed, revolutionary, insufficient, precise, rarely, always.

Quantifiers and Data: Words like all, none, most, 75%, a majority provide critical scale and scope.

The "Text-Whisperer" Drill:

Procedure: Take a highlighter and a dense paragraph. Read through it quickly and highlight **only the 5-7 words** that you believe are absolutely essential to the paragraph's core meaning. You will be forced to ignore the filler and isolate the signal. Do this repeatedly to train your brain to automatically filter for meaning.

3. Reading for Purpose: The Spectrum of Engagement

An elite reader does not have one reading speed; they have a gearbox. They shift their approach based on the text and their purpose for reading it. Skimming and sliding are specific gears in that box.

Gear 1: Analytical Reading (The Low Gear - For Deep Study)

Purpose: To achieve deep, comprehensive understanding and long-term retention of complex, unfamiliar, or critically important material (e.g., legal contracts, scientific papers, core textbooks).

Technique: This is **not** skimming. This is slow, careful reading. You read every word. You pause to look up unfamiliar terms. You take detailed notes. You re-read difficult passages. You may use a pointer for focus, but your pace is deliberate.

The Role of Skimming: Skimming is used here as a **pre-reading tool** (the 60-second map) and a **post-reading review tool** (skimming your notes and the headings to reinforce the structure).

Gear 3: Comprehensive Reading (The Cruising Gear - For Leisure and General Learning)

Purpose: To enjoy a novel, understand a news article, or learn from a non-fiction book for general knowledge.

Technique: This is your practiced speed reading mode. You use a pacer, read in phrases, and maintain a good pace (400-800 WPM) while aiming for strong comprehension. You do not stop for every unknown word; you infer meaning from context.

The Role of Skimming: Skimming is used here to **check in**. If your mind wanders, you might skim a few sentences to get back on track. You might skim ahead in a novel if suspense is overwhelming, or skim a familiar section of a non-fiction book to review.

Gear 5: Strategic Skimming (The High Gear - For Triage and Information Gathering)

Purpose: To quickly evaluate a text's relevance, extract only the specific information you need, or review a large volume of material in a very short time (e.g., researching on the web, going through emails, reviewing reports before a meeting, studying right before an exam).

Technique: This is pure **sliding and skimming**. You are in a high-state of alertness, scanning for specific keywords and ideas. You use your finger in a rapid "S" or "Z" pattern down the page. You read only:

The first and last sentence of each paragraph.

All headings and subheadings.

Bolded, italicized, and listed text.

Names, dates, and statistics.
You are actively constructing understanding from these key pieces, filling in the gaps with inference and prior knowledge. Comprehension is not 100%, but it is sufficient for the purpose at hand.

The Integrated Skimming Protocol:

Define Your Purpose: Before you touch the text, ask: "Why am I reading this? What do I need to get out of it?" This determines your gear.

Pre-Read (Skim): Spend 60 seconds with Gear 5 to create your mental map, regardless of your ultimate goal.

Engage: Shift into the appropriate gear (1, 3, or 5) and read.

Review (Skim Again): When finished, spend 30 seconds skimming the headings, your notes, and the conclusion to cement the structure in your memory.

Conclusion: The Strategic Reader

Skimming is the mark of a strategic and confident reader. It is the recognition that not all words are created equal and that not all texts deserve equal attention. By mastering the art of sliding and skimming, you move from being a passive consumer of text to an active director of your cognitive resources. You learn to allocate your precious time and attention where they will have the greatest return on investment. This skill empowers you to navigate the information-dense modern world not with anxiety, but with calm, controlled efficiency. You are no longer overwhelmed by volume; you are empowered by strategy.

13

Beyond Speed: The Symbiosis of Rapid Reading and Deep Retention

---

The True Goal of Reading

Speed without understanding is noise. Pace without retention is a forgotten journey. The ultimate purpose of reading is not to see words quickly, but to acquire, integrate, and recall knowledge efficiently. This chapter addresses the most crucial concern of the aspiring speed reader: "If I read so fast, how will I remember anything?"

The answer lies in rejecting the false dichotomy between speed and memory. They are not opposing forces; they are synergistic partners. The techniques that enable speed reading—enhanced focus, chunking ideas, and reducing cognitive clutter—are the very same conditions that create an optimal environment for memory encoding. This chapter will bridge the gap between velocity and longevity in learning. We will explore how to leverage the speed reading process itself as a powerful memory primer, and then introduce a suite of advanced cognitive strategies—from ancient visualization techniques to modern note-taking systems—designed to lock information into your long-term memory. You will learn that reading faster can actually mean remembering more, if you know how to harness the process correctly.

1. Linking Speed Reading with Memory: The Cognitive Advantage

The connection between speed and memory is rooted in the fundamental workings of attention and cognitive load.

The Focus Factor: Slow, plodding reading allows for mind-wandering. Each time your mind drifts and you have to re-read, you break the fragile chain of concentration necessary for memory formation. Speed reading, by demanding intense, sustained focus, keeps your brain fully engaged with the material. This heightened state of attention is the primary prerequisite for moving information from short-term to long-term memory.

Chunking for Memory: We've discussed chunking for reading speed, but it is also a core memory principle. Your working memory can hold only about 4-7 discrete items. By reading the phrase "the theory of relativity" as one chunk (one item) instead of three separate words (three items), you free up cognitive space. This allows you to remember the relationship between ideas rather than struggling to remember the ideas themselves. You are remembering concepts, not words.

Reducing Internal Distraction: Subvocalization and regression are forms of cognitive static. They create internal noise that interferes with the clean encoding of information. By minimizing these, the signal (the author's core ideas) comes through more clearly and is more easily recorded by the hippocampus, the brain's key memory formation center.

The Role of Purpose: Speed reading is inherently active reading. You are not passive; you are hunting for meaning, structure, and key ideas. This active engagement is a form of "deep processing," which is the most effective way to ensure long-term retention. You are not just reading; you are having a conversation with the text.

2. Visualization & Association Techniques: Building Memory Palaces

Memory champions don't have better brains; they have better strategies. They use the brain's innate strengths—its ability to remember images, spaces, and absurdity—to store abstract information.

The Visualization Principle: Convert abstract concepts into concrete, vivid mental images. The more detailed, colorful, and exaggerated the image, the more memorable it becomes.

Example: To remember that Einstein developed the theory of relativity, don't remember the words. Instead, picture a wild-haired Einstein (A) riding a beam of light (B) and holding a clock that is melting (C: time dilation). This single, bizarre image encodes the who, the what, and a key detail.

The Link and Story Method: Connect a series of ideas or items into a ridiculous, illogical story. The narrative structure provides a sequence, and the absurdity makes it sticky.

Example: To remember the key points of an article on economics (inflation, interest rates, supply chain), you might visualize: A giant, inflated (inflation) balloon (a) is floating up to the sky, but it's tied down with ropes made of coins (interest rates weighing it down) (b), and the coins are being minted by a squeaky, rusty conveyor belt (supply chain issues) (c).

The Memory Palace (Method of Loci): This ancient, powerful technique leverages your superb memory for physical locations.

Choose a Palace: Visualize a place you know intimately (your home, your route to work).

Identify Loci: Select specific, sequential locations within this place (your front door, the coat rack, the lamp, the sofa).

Place Images: As you read, convert key ideas into vivid images and "place" them at each locus. To recall, simply take a mental walk through your palace and "see" the ideas.

Application for Reading: After skimming a chapter, identify the 5-7 key concepts. Build your images for them and place them in your palace. This creates a powerful, non-linear retrieval structure for the material.

3. Mind Maps and Note-Taking: Externalizing Understanding

Note-taking is not about transcription; it's about translation. You are translating the author's linear structure into your own personal, connected web of understanding.

Why Linear Notes Fail: Traditional, sequential notes often fail to capture the relationships between ideas. They encourage passive copying and can be difficult to review.

Mind Mapping for Speed Readers:

The Process: After reading a section (using your speed reading skills), put the book down. Take a blank sheet of paper and draw a central image representing the main topic. For every major branch, draw a thick line and write a key concept (using 1-2 words, in CAPITALS). Add smaller branches for details, facts, and examples. Use images, symbols, and colors liberally.

The Synergy: This activity forces your brain to do the critical work of identification, prioritization, and synthesis. It is the ultimate comprehension check. The spatial and visual nature of a mind map mirrors how your brain stores information, making it incredibly efficient for review.

The Cornell Note-Taking System:
This structured format is ideal for dense, academic material.

Cue Column (Left Side): After reading and taking notes in the main section, you go back and write key questions, keywords, or prompts in this narrow column. This is an active recall trigger.

Note-Taking Area (Right Side): Use this area during or immediately after reading to capture key ideas, using your own words and shorthand. Focus on concepts, not sentences.

Summary (Bottom): After you're finished, write a brief 2-3 sentence summary of the entire page's notes. This is the final, powerful act of synthesis.

The Speed Reading Link: The process of creating Cornell Notes—especially formulating questions and writing summaries—is a form of deep processing that ensures the information is thoroughly encoded.

4. Review and Recall Methods: The Forgetting Curve and Spaced Repetition

Memory is not a recording; it is a process. Forgetting is natural, but it can be strategically defeated.

Ebbinghaus's Forgetting Curve: Hermann Ebbinghaus demonstrated that we forget exponentially if we do not review information. We can lose over 50% of what we've learned within an hour and 80% within a week without review.

Strategic Review via Spaced Repetition: This is the scientifically-proven method to break the forgetting curve. It involves reviewing information at increasingly longer intervals, just as you are about to forget it. This powerfully strengthens the neural pathway each time.

The Algorithm for Memory:

First Review: 10-20 minutes after finishing reading (e.g., create your mind map or Cornell summary).

Second Review: Later the same day (e.g., glance over your notes for 5 minutes).

Third Review: The next morning.

Fourth Review: One week later.

Fifth Review: One month later.

After this, the information is likely consolidated into long-term memory.

Active Recall: The Golden Principle

The most effective review is not re-reading your notes or the text. It is active recall—forcing your brain to retrieve the information from memory without looking.

Techniques:

After reading, close the book and write down everything you can remember.

Use the Cue Column in your Cornell Notes: Cover the notes section and try to recite the details based only on the cue.

Explain the concept to someone else (or to yourself out loud).

Use flashcards (physical or digital like Anki) that leverage spaced repetition.

The Integrated Memory Protocol for a Speed Reader:

Pre-Read (Skim): 60 seconds to create a mental map. (Activates prior knowledge and primes the brain).

Speed Read: Read the section at your optimal pace using a pacer and chunking. (Encodes information efficiently under high focus).

Immediate Recall & Note-Taking (within 20 mins): Put the text away. Create a mind map or Cornell Note from memory. This is the most critical step for retention.

First Review (same day): Spend 5 minutes looking at your notes and trying to recall the details with active recall.

Spaced Repetition: Schedule brief reviews at increasing intervals (next day, week, month).

Conclusion: The Virtuous Cycle of Learning

When you combine speed reading with deliberate memory strategies, you create a virtuous cycle. Speed reading provides the focused, efficient intake of information. The memory techniques then act upon this high-quality input, organizing, storing, and strengthening it. The result is not just faster reading, but faster, deeper, and more permanent *learning*.

You are no longer just a reader; you are a builder of knowledge. You are constructing a sophisticated, interconnected web of understanding in your mind, one that is easily accessible and durable. This is the true power of reading—not to race through text, but to capture wisdom.

14

The Adaptive Reader: Mastering Speed Reading for Different Materials

One Size Does Not Fit All

An expert driver does not use the same technique on a slick racetrack, a rocky mountain trail, and a crowded city street. They understand that the vehicle's capabilities must be matched to the demands of the terrain. Similarly, an expert reader does not have a single, fixed reading speed. They possess a flexible repertoire of strategies and understand precisely which to deploy based on the material in front of them.

Attempting to read a dense textbook at the same speed as a light novel is as inefficient as reading a light novel at the same painstaking pace as a textbook. This chapter is your guide to becoming an adaptive reader. We will dissect the unique challenges and optimal strategies for four key reading environments: academic texts, periodicals, digital content, and leisure reading. You will learn how to dynamically balance the seemingly opposing forces of skimming and deep reading, transforming yourself from a one-trick reader into a versatile knowledge athlete, capable of conquering any text with precision and efficiency.

1. Conquering the Citadel: Strategies for Textbooks & Exams

Academic material is the ultimate test of a speed reader's skill. The goal here is not just speed, but deep comprehension, critical analysis, and long-term retention.

The Pre-Read Reconnaissance (SQ3R Method): Never dive straight in. First, conduct a strategic survey.

Survey: Spend 5-10 minutes skimming the entire chapter. Read the title, headings, subheadings, introductory and summary paragraphs, review questions, charts, graphs, and bolded terms. Your goal is to build a detailed mental map of the content's structure and key concepts.

Question: Turn each heading and subheading into a question. "The Causes of the French Revolution" becomes "What were the causes of the French Revolution?" This frames your reading as an active search for answers, dramatically increasing engagement and retention.

Now, Read: Only now do you begin to read. Use your speed reading techniques—chunking, pacing, minimizing subvocalization—but be prepared to shift gears. Your pace will be variable.

Variable Pace Control: This is the key skill for academic reading.

Accelerate: Speed up through explanations of concepts you already know, familiar examples, and transitional paragraphs.

Decelerate: Slow down significantly for definitions of key terms, statements of principle, formulas, and complex arguments. This is where you might switch from phrase-reading to word-by-word reading to ensure perfect understanding.

The Annotation System: Engage in a dialogue with the text. Use a pencil or digital highlighter with a purpose.

Marginalia: Write brief summaries, questions, or reactions in the margins. Use symbols (!, ?, →, ★) to mark important points, confusing passages, or connections to other ideas.

Strategic Highlighting: Never highlight more than 10-15% of the text. Only highlight the absolute core: a key term and its definition, a pivotal thesis statement, or a crucial piece of evidence. The act of deciding what to highlight is a powerful cognitive filter.

Exam-Specific Reading: When faced with exam passages or questions, your strategy shifts.

For Questions: Read the question stem first. Underline key command words ("compare," "contrast," "analyze," "define"). This primes your brain to search for specific information.

For Passages: Skim the questions first to know what to look for. Then, read the passage actively, using your finger to maintain focus and pace, mentally tagging information that seems relevant to the questions you saw.

2. Staying Informed: Reading Newspapers & Magazines

The goal here is efficient information triage: quickly identifying what is important, relevant, and interesting amidst a high volume of content.

The Article Inverted Pyramid: News and magazine articles are famously structured with the most important information first (the who, what, when, where, why) followed by supporting details and background. Leverage this.

The Strategic Skim:

Headline and Subhead: Understand the core topic.

First 1-2 Paragraphs: This contains the lead and will give you 80% of the crucial information.

The Final Paragraph: Often contains a concluding thought or forward-looking statement.

Scan the Body: Let your eyes slide down the column, catching any bolded names, quotes, or statistics. Only slow down if a particular detail grabs your interest.

The Section Triage: Before you even start on articles, skim the entire newspaper or magazine. Read the table of contents. Understand what each section contains. Decide which sections are a priority and which can be skipped or skimmed lightly. This prevents you from wasting time on content that doesn't serve your purpose.

3. The Digital Dilemma: Digital vs. Print Reading Differences

Reading on a screen is a fundamentally different cognitive experience than reading on paper. Understanding these differences allows you to adapt your strategy.

The Challenges of Digital Reading:

Hyperlinks: These are decision points that fracture attention and lead to distraction. The temptation to "just click this one link" is a major productivity killer.

Notifications: The constant potential for alerts from other apps creates a state of "continuous partial attention," deeply undermining focus.

Screen Fatigue: Eye strain from backlighting (glare) and blue light can reduce reading endurance.

Shallowing Effect: Studies suggest we tend to read more superficially on screens, skimming rather than engaging in deep reading.

Strategies for Digital Dominance:

Declare War on Distraction: Use browser extensions (like StayFocusd, Freedom) to block distracting websites and notifications during reading sessions. Put your phone in another room.

Curate Your View: Use reader modes (available in most browsers and apps like Pocket) that strip away ads, menus, and other clutter, presenting text in a clean, customizable, print-like format.

The "Why" Test: Before clicking any hyperlink, ask yourself: "Is this link essential to my understanding right now?" If not, don't click. If it is, consider opening it in a new tab to read after you finish your current text.

The Digital Pointer: Your finger or cursor becomes even more critical on a screen to maintain focus and guide your eyes through the visual noise.

4. The Masterful Balance: Skimming vs. Deep Reading

The adaptive reader is a maestro, conducting the orchestra of their skills to create the perfect performance for each piece of music.

The Spectrum of Reading: Imagine your reading approach as a spectrum. On one end is Superficial Skimming (getting the absolute gist). On the other end is Analytical Deep Reading (critical, line-by-line analysis). Most of your reading will fall somewhere in between.

How to Choose Your Gear:

Skim (Gear 5) When: You are previewing, reviewing, researching a specific fact, triaging emails/news, or reading something of low importance.

Speed Read (Gear 3-4) When: You are reading for general comprehension and enjoyment—novels, general non-fiction, blogs, reports where you need the full picture efficiently.

Deep Read (Gear 1-2) When: You are studying complex, unfamiliar, or critically important material (legal documents, poetry, technical manuals, core textbooks).

The Two-Pass Technique: For material that is important but not worthy of a full deep read, use this efficient method:

The Skim Pass (First Pass): Read the entire piece at a high speed (your Gear 4). Your goal is to understand the structure, main argument, and key conclusions. As you do this, make light mental or physical marks next to sections that seem complex, important, or unfamiliar.

The Deep Dive Pass (Second Pass): Now, only go back and re-read the sections you marked at a slower, more analytical pace (Gear 2). You have already built the framework; now you are installing the intricate details where they are needed. This saves immense time compared to reading everything slowly.

Conclusion: The Reader as Strategist

Becoming a speed reader is not about achieving a single, blistering top speed. It is about developing reading fluency—the ability to effortlessly adjust your pace, strategy, and focus to align with your purpose for reading and the nature of the text itself.

The true measure of your skill is not your words-per-minute on a novel, but your ability to instantly diagnose a reading challenge and select the perfect tool from your mental toolbox. It is the difference between being a hammer—for which every problem looks like a nail—and a master carpenter with a full belt of tools, each designed for a specific, expert purpose. By mastering the adaptive strategies in this chapter, you cease to be a passive consumer of text and become an active, strategic, and utterly efficient master of information.

15

Overcoming Common Obstacles - Mastering Your Mind, Body, and Text

Reading is a journey. Like any worthwhile expedition, the path is not always smooth. You will encounter internal storms of distraction, steep cliffs of dense prose, and the physical fatigue of a long trek. The difference between a frustrated reader and a masterful one is not the absence of these obstacles, but the possession of a well-stocked toolkit to navigate them.

This chapter is your toolkit. We will move from the internal battle for focus, to the intellectual challenge of complex texts, and finally to the physical care of your most important reading instrument—your eyes. By the end, you will be equipped to transform reading from a potential chore into a consistently rewarding and sustainable practice.

The Lure of the Ping - Dealing with Distractions

In the 21st century, the greatest threat to deep reading is not illiteracy, but constant interruption. Our environments and our devices are engineered to splinter our attention. Conquering distraction is the first step toward reading mastery.

Understanding the Enemy: Internal vs. External Distractions

External Distractions: These are stimuli from your environment. The ping of a phone notification, the chatter of colleagues, the blare of a television, clutter on your desk, or even a room that's too hot or too cold.

Internal Distractions: These originate from within your own mind. Anxiety about an upcoming deadline, a mental grocery list, daydreaming, fatigue, or emotional turmoil. These are often more pernicious because you can't simply turn them off.

Strategies for a Distraction-Proof Reading Session

1. Curate Your Environment (Taming the External):

The Phone: The Arch-Nemesis: This is your biggest battle. Do not simply silence it; place it in another room. If you need it for a dictionary, enable "Do Not Disturb" or "Focus Mode," ensuring only essential notifications can break through. Consider apps like Forest or Freedom that block distracting apps for set periods.

Designate a "Reading Zone": Your brain associates certain places with certain activities. If you always read in a specific chair, at a clean desk, or in a particular corner of the library, your mind will begin to shift into "reading mode" more quickly when you're there.

Control the Auditory Landscape: If silence is too stark, use sound to block sound. Noise-canceling headphones are a superb investment. Use them to listen to ambient soundscapes (rainfall, coffee shop murmur, white noise) or instrumental music (classical, lo-fi, film scores). Lyrics often hijack the language-processing part of your brain, making them counterproductive.

Communicate Your Boundaries: If you're reading at home with others, a simple "I'm going to read for the next hour, I'd appreciate no interruptions" sets a clear expectation.

2. Train Your Mind (Quieting the Internal):

The "Mind Dump" Technique: Before you begin reading, take exactly three minutes to write down everything swirling in your head—tasks, worries, ideas. Get it out on paper and promise yourself you'll deal with it after your reading session. This clears valuable mental RAM.

Set a Clear Intention: Don't just pick up a book vaguely. State a purpose. "I am reading this chapter to understand the causes of the French Revolution." This gives your mind a mission and a point of focus to return to when it wanders.

Embrace the Wandering Mind (Gently): Your mind will wander. This is normal. The key is not to get frustrated, but to develop a gentle, non-judgmental awareness of it. When you notice you've been thinking about your weekend plans for the last three paragraphs, simply note it ("Ah, wandering") and guide your attention back to the text. This is a rep, like a bicep curl for your focus muscle.

Forging Mental Steel - Improving Focus and Discipline

Focus and discipline are not mystical traits you're born with; they are muscles that are built through consistent practice. Discipline is making the right choice; focus is maintaining that choice over time.

Building the Focus Muscle: Practical Training Regimens

1. The Pomodoro Technique:

This is arguably the most effective method for building reading focus. The principle is simple:

Set a timer for **25 minutes**.

Read with complete, undivided attention until the timer rings.

Take a mandatory, **5-minute break**. Stand up, walk around, look out a window, hydrate.

After four "Pomodoros," take a longer break (15-20 minutes).

Why it works: It transforms an intimidating multi-hour reading session into a series of manageable sprints. Knowing a break is coming soon makes it easier to resist the urge to check your phone now.

2. Start Small and Scale Up:

If 25 minutes feels impossible, start with 10. Or even 5. The goal is to succeed at a small interval of deep focus. Success builds confidence. The next day, try 12 minutes. Gradually, you will expand your capacity for sustained attention.

3. Active Reading as a Focus Tool:

Passive reading is a fast track to zoning out. Force your brain to engage by making reading an active process.

Hold a Pen or Highlighter: Even if you don't use it, the physical object keeps your hands engaged and signals intent.

Margin Notes: Write brief reactions, questions, or summaries in the margins. Argue with the author! Agree with them! This is a conversation.

Summarize Paragraphs: After reading a dense paragraph, pause and verbally summarize it in one sentence. This ensures you've processed it before moving on.

4. Track Your Progress and Reward Yourself:

Maintain a simple reading log. Note down how many Pomodoros you completed or how many pages you read with deep focus. This tangible record of progress is highly motivating. Pair your reading session with a reward: "After I finish these two chapters, I can have that cup of coffee and watch one episode of my show."

Taming the Tough Stuff - Handling Technical or Dense Texts

A complex textbook, a dense academic paper, a legal document, or a philosophical treatise—these texts are intellectual marathons. They require a different strategy than a novel. Your goal is not speed; it is **comprehension.**

A Strategic Approach to Difficult Reading

1. Pre-Reading: Scouting the Territory

Never jump headfirst into a dense text. First, scout it out.

Read the Abstract, Introduction, and Conclusion: These sections contain the author's main thesis, structure, and summary of findings. You are building a mental framework.

Scan Headings and Subheadings: Understand the architecture of the argument. Look at any charts, graphs, or images. Read the captions.

Identify Key Terms: Skim for bolded words, definitions, and repeated terminology. These are the pillars of the text. Look them up now if you're unsure.

2. The First Pass: Reading for the Gist

Your first read-through should be done with the explicit permission to not understand everything. Read a section at a time (a heading to the next heading) with the goal of answering: "What is the big idea here?" Don't get bogged down by a confusing equation or a convoluted sentence. Mark it with a pencil and move on. Often, the broader context will make the difficult passage clearer on the second pass.

3. The Second Pass: The Deep Dig

Now, return to the beginning. This is where you engage in close reading.

Tackle One Paragraph at a Time: Read a paragraph. Stop. Can you explain it in your own words? If not, re-read it. Break down complex sentences into their core components (Subject, Verb, Object).

Paraphrase Aloud: Explaining the concept aloud, as if to a student, forces you to confront whether you truly understand it.

Look Everything Up: Now is the time to investigate those marked passages, look up unfamiliar terms, and follow footnotes. Create a personal glossary if needed.

4. Utilize Supplementary Resources:

Find a Summary or Guide: For canonical texts, websites like SparkNotes or JSTOR often have summaries and analyses that can provide crucial context.

Talk About It: Discuss the text with a friend, classmate, or online forum. Explaining your confusion often leads to clarity.

Connect to What You Know: Relate the new, complex information to concepts you already understand. Analogies are powerful tools for building bridges in your mind.

The Care and Keeping of Your Eyes - Avoiding Eye Strain and Fatigue

Reading is a physically demanding act for your eyes. Ignoring their health leads to fatigue, headaches, and an aversion to reading. This is not just about comfort; it's about building a sustainable lifelong habit.

The Enemies of Ocular Health

Digital Screens (Blue Light & Glare): Emit blue light that can disrupt sleep patterns and cause strain. The constant focus on a single, glowing plane is exhausting.

Poor Lighting: Reading in dim light forces your pupils to dilate excessively, while harsh, direct light creates glare and shadows, both causing fatigue.

Static Posture and Lack of Blinking: We blink significantly less often when staring at a screen or book, leading to dry, irritated eyes. Remaining frozen in one position creates muscle tension.

An Ergonomics and Eye-Care Checklist

1. Optimize Your Setup:

Lighting is Key: The best light for reading is **natural, indirect daylight.** For artificial light, ensure your room is evenly lit to avoid a bright pool of light on the page surrounded by darkness. Use a soft, warm-toned desk lamp directed onto your page, not your eyes.

Screen Hygiene:

Enable Night Shift / Blue Light Filter: Schedule this on your devices to automatically reduce blue light in the evenings.

Adjust Brightness and Contrast: Your screen brightness should roughly match the brightness of your surroundings. Avoid reading on a blazingly bright screen in a dark room.

Increase Text Size: Don't squint. Make the text large enough to read comfortably from your normal reading position.

Perfect Your Posture: Don't read lying down or slouched over. Sit upright with your back supported. Hold your book or device so that you are looking slightly down at it, about 20 inches from your eyes. This is the most natural and least stressful angle for your eyes and neck.

2. Practice Active Eye Care:

The 20-20-20 Rule: This is the golden rule. **Every 20 minutes, look at something at least 20 feet away for at least 20 seconds.** This simple act relaxes the focusing muscle inside your eye and is the single most effective thing you can do to prevent digital eye strain. Set a timer if you have to.

Conscious Blinking: Remind yourself to blink fully and frequently to rewet your eyes.

Hydrate: Drink water throughout your reading session. Dehydration affects your entire body, including your eyes.

3. Know When to Stop:

Listening to your body is not a sign of weakness. If your eyes are burning, your head is throbbing, and you can't concentrate, you are no longer absorbing information. The most productive thing you can do is **stop**. Close your eyes, take a walk, or switch to an audiobook for a while. Sustainable reading is a marathon, not a sprint.

Synthesis: The Resilient Reader

The obstacles of distraction, lack of focus, difficult texts, and physical strain are interconnected. A tired mind is more easily distracted. A distracting environment prevents the deep focus needed for technical texts. Eye strain will break your discipline.

By employing the strategies in this chapter holistically, you build a system of resilience. You create a distraction-free sanctuary, you train your focus like an athlete, you approach difficult texts like a strategist, and you treat your body with the respect it deserves.

The path to reading mastery is not never falling, but learning how to get up, dust yourself off, and continue the journey with wiser, stronger eyes. Now, turn the page, and begin.

16
The Architecture of Achievement - Your Daily Practice Plan

Knowledge without application is like a book that is never opened. The strategies, techniques, and mindsets explored in this guide are inert theory until they are woven into the fabric of your daily life. This chapter is the practical blueprint for that integration.

We will move from a gentle, 7-day onboarding routine designed to build confidence, to a transformative 30-day challenge that solidifies reading as a core habit, and finally to the long-term practices that transmute habit into mastery. We will also define what true progress looks like, moving beyond mere page counts to meaningful, personal growth.

Laying the Foundation - The 7-Day Beginner Routine

The goal of this first week is not to read for hours on end or to finish War and Peace. The goal is **consistent, focused engagement.** We are building the ritual itself, making it a non-negotiable part of your day, like brushing your teeth.

Guiding Philosophy: Start so small that success is inevitable. Consistency trumps volume.

The Daily Structure (20-30 minutes total)

5 Min: Preparation & Mindset (The "Why")

15-20 Min: Active Reading (The "What")

2 Min: Reflection & Logging (The "Progress")

Day 1: The Ritual of Preparation

Task: Your only reading task today is to choose your book. Select something engaging and accessible—a popular nonfiction book on a subject you love, a highly-recommended novel, a short story collection.

Practice: Establish your "Reading Launch Sequence." Find your spot. Silence your phone and place it in another room. Gather a glass of water, a notebook, and a pen. Set a timer for 15 minutes. Sit down. Take three deep breaths. This is the ritual. You may not even read the full 15 minutes. The success condition is completing the ritual.

Day 2: The First Sprint

Task: Execute your full Reading Launch Sequence. Start your timer and read for 15 minutes. When the timer goes off, stop immediately, even if you're in the middle of a sentence.

Why: This teaches your brain that this is a focused, time-bound activity, not an open-ended chore. Stopping while you're still engaged makes it easier to start again tomorrow.

Day 3: Taming the Internal Chatter

Task: Repeat the sequence. Today, during your 15 minutes, notice your mind wandering. Each time it does, gently label the thought ("planning," "worrying," "memory") and guide your focus back to the text. Do not judge yourself. This is practice.

Reflection: After your session, jot down in your notebook: "What was the most common type of distraction today?"

Day 4: Active Reading - The Question

Task: As you read today, hold one question in your mind: **"What is the one key idea the author is presenting in this section?"** Your pen is your tool. Underline a single sentence that seems to answer this question.

Reflection: In your notebook, write that one sentence in your own words.

Day 5: Active Reading - The Connection

Task: Today's question is: **"How does this connect to something I already know or have experienced?"** Look for a personal connection, however small.

Reflection: Write down that connection. "This character's dilemma reminds me of when I..." or "This fact about gravity explains why..."

Day 6: Integrating the 20-20-20 Rule

Task: Set a timer for 15 minutes. Every 5 minutes, when the timer vibrates or beeps, practice the 20-20-20 rule: look away from the page and focus on something 20 feet away for 20 seconds. Then return to reading.

Why: You are now layering in sustainable habit #1: eye care.

Day 7: Review and Consolidation

Task: Complete your full ritual. Read for 15 focused minutes.

Reflection: This is your weekly review. Look back at your notebook entries for the past week. Write one paragraph answering: "What did I enjoy or learn from this week's reading sessions? How did it feel to do this consistently?" Acknowledge your success.

Building Momentum - The 30-Day Reading Challenge

You have built the foundation. Now, we will expand the structure, intensify the focus, and solidify reading as a dominant positive force in your daily routine. The goal of this month is **transformation through habit stacking and skill development.**

The Non-Negotiable Daily Core (Now 30-45 minutes):

5 Min: Preparation, Mindset, & "Mind Dump"

25-35 Min: Active Reading using the Pomodoro Technique (25-min focus, 5-min break)

5 Min: Reflection, Logging, & Previewing the next session

Week 1: Habit Stacking & Environment Optimization

Focus: Anchor your reading time to an existing habit (e.g., "After I pour my morning coffee, I will read for one Pomodoro" or "Right after I get into bed, I will read for 25 minutes").

Challenge: Perfect your environment. Experiment with different lighting. Find the perfect ambient noise track (e.g., coffivity.com, ambient-mixer.com). Ensure your chair and reading position are ergonomic.

Week 2: Technique Expansion

Focus: Introduce a new active reading technique every other day.

Day 1-2: The Marginalia. Write questions, reactions, and summaries in the margins (or in your notebook if it's a library book).

Day 3-4: The Socratic Interrogation. Pause every few pages and ask: "What is the author assuming here? What evidence are they providing? Is it convincing?"

Day 5-7: The One-Sentence Summary. After each reading session, force yourself to distill the main point of what you read into a single, well-crafted sentence in your journal.

Week 3: Tackling Density

Focus: Apply the strategies from Chapter 7 to a deliberately more challenging text. This could be a chapter from a dense nonfiction book, a long-form magazine article, or a technical paper related to your field.

Challenge: Practice pre-reading. Before you start your timer, spend 3 minutes scanning headings, introductions, and conclusions. Then, do your two-pass read: first for gist, second for detail.

Week 4: Synthesis and Integration

Focus: Connect your reading to other parts of your life.

Challenge:

Explain it: Explain a key concept from your reading to a friend, partner, or even just to your camera phone.

Apply it: Find one small, actionable idea from your reading and implement it this week. Did you read a book on productivity? Try the "2-minute rule." A book on philosophy? Practice a Stoic exercise for a day.

Cross-pollinate: If you're reading fiction, listen to an interview with the author or a related podcast. If you're reading history, look at a map from the era.

The Lifelong Practice - Long-Term Habits for Mastery

After 30 days, reading is a habit. Mastery is what happens over the next 30 months. Mastery is not a destination but a direction—a continuous commitment to refinement and depth.

1. Develop a Personal Canon:
Move from random reading to intentional exploration. Let books lead to other books. Read deeply within a genre or subject you love, creating a web of understanding. Simultaneously, read broadly outside your comfort zone to challenge your assumptions and foster intellectual humility.

2. Cultivate a Slow Reading Practice:
Balance your diet of new books with re-reading. Your favorite books will reveal new layers to you at different stages of your life. Mastery involves returning to foundational texts to mine them for deeper meaning you weren't equipped to see the first time.

3. Join the Conversation:
Reading is solitary, but understanding is social.

Join or start a book club.

Follow and engage with critics and authors online.

Write reviews on platforms like Goodreads or a personal blog. Formulating a critique for an audience forces a deeper level of analysis.

4. The Curated Input System:
A master reader is also a master chooser. Develop a system for managing your "To-Read" list (TBR). Use tools like Goodreads to track recommendations. Regularly prune your TBR to ensure it

reflects your evolving interests, not just past whims.

5. Teach What You Learn:

The ultimate test of mastery is the ability to teach. Volunteer, mentor, or simply make a point of sharing your insights with others. Teaching consolidates knowledge and exposes the gaps in your understanding, guiding your future reading.

The Map and The Compass - How to Measure Progress

If you don't know how to measure progress, you will never know if you're improving. Ditch the simplistic metric of "books read per year." True progress is multidimensional.

Quantitative Metrics (The Map):

These are the objective numbers. Track them in a simple spreadsheet or journal.

Consistency: Number of days read per week/month. (Goal: Consistency > 90%).

Time Invested: Total minutes of focused reading per day/week. (Seeing this number grow is incredibly motivating).

Pomodoros Completed: A measure of deep work sessions.

Pages Read: Useful, but secondary to time invested.

Qualitative Metrics (The Compass):

These are the subjective, far more important measures of true progress. Reflect on these in your journal weekly or monthly.

Depth of Understanding: Do you find yourself making connections to other books, ideas, and life experiences more easily? Can you explain the concepts to someone else?

Reduction in Distraction: How long does it take you to achieve deep focus? Has it gotten easier to ignore your phone and internal chatter?

Stamina: Can you comfortably engage in two or three Pomodoro sessions back-to-back without mental fatigue?

Vocabulary & Expression: Are you noticing new words entering your active vocabulary? Is your own writing and speaking becoming more precise and nuanced?

Joy and Anticipation: Do you look forward to your reading time? Has it shifted from a "should" to a "get to"?

Critical Engagement: Are you moving from passive absorption ("What does it say?") to active interrogation ("Why did the author choose this structure? Is this argument valid? What is missing?").

The Mastery Dashboard:

Once a month, conduct a personal review. Look at your quantitative data and journal reflections. Ask yourself:

What went well this month?

What was my biggest insight from reading?

What obstacle did I overcome?

Based on this, what is my focus for next month? (e.g., "Increase time to 45 min/day," "Try a denser book," "Join an online book discussion")

This process turns reading from a passive hobby into an active practice of self-development. You are not just reading books; you are building a richer, more thoughtful, and more capable mind, one page, one day, one insight at a time. The journey to mastery begins not with a single leap, but with the decision to take the first step today.

17

The End of the Beginning – Your Lifelong Reading Journey

We began this journey with a simple, powerful question: What if you could not only read faster, but also understand more, retain longer, and enjoy the process more deeply?

You have now moved from question to possession. You are equipped with the tools, strategies, and mindset shifts that demystify the art and science of effective reading. This conclusion is not an end, but a commissioning. It is a synthesis of the path you have walked and a map for the road ahead. Here, we will consolidate the techniques you've mastered, translate them into a practical blueprint for your daily life, and finally, reframe what it truly means to become a lifelong learner and reader.

Part 1: The Master Toolkit - A Summary of Techniques Learned

You have built a comprehensive reading framework. Let's review its core components, not as isolated tricks, but as an integrated system.

I. The Foundational Mindset Shifts:

Reading is a Skill, Not a Talent: You now know that reading can be systematically improved with practice, like playing a musical instrument or a sport. This empowers you to take ownership of your growth.

Comprehension over Velocity: The ultimate goal is not to see words faster, but to process ideas more efficiently. Speed is the beneficial byproduct of clarity and focus, not the other way around.

Active over Passive Reading: You have transitioned from being a passive recipient of information to an active engager—a critic, a questioner, a connector. The text is now a conversation partner.

II. The Mechanical Engine: Speed Techniques

Eliminating Subvocalization: You learned to quiet the inner whisper, allowing your brain to process ideas at its natural, vastly superior speed, rather than being chained to the pace of speech.

Expanding Peripheral Vision: You practice using your foveal and parafoveal vision to take in groups of words (chunks) with a single fixation, reducing the stop-and-start "saccades" that slow down inefficient readers.

Using a Pacer: Whether your finger, a pen, or a digital highlight bar, you possess the simplest and most powerful tool to guide your eyes, maintain rhythm, prevent regression, and steadily increase pace.

Reducing Fixation Time: You train your brain to process the meaning of a word group almost instantly and move on, building momentum and flow.

III. The Cognitive Framework: Comprehension & Retention

Pre-Reading & Previewing: You no longer dive in blind. You scout the territory by reading headings, subheadings, introductions, conclusions, and summary paragraphs to build a mental scaffold for the details to come.

Setting a Purpose (PSR): Before you read, you ask, "Why am I reading this? What do I want to get out of it?" This simple question primes your brain to seek and retain relevant information.

The Questioning Mind: You constantly interrogate the text. "What is the main idea here?" "What is the evidence?" "How does this connect?" This active engagement is the glue of memory.

Post-Reading Synthesis: You solidify learning by summarizing what you read in your own words, either verbally, in writing, or through a mind map. This is where knowledge is transferred from short-term to long-term memory.

IV. The Sustainability Protocol: Focus & Health

Managing Distractions: You create a dedicated reading environment, use tools like the Pomodoro Technique for focused sprints, and practice mindfulness to gently return your focus when it wanders.

Preventing Fatigue: The 20-20-20 rule and proper ergonomics are now non-negotiable parts of your practice, ensuring your physical comfort and long-term eye health.

Building a Habit: You understand the power of consistency, using micro-habits and ritual to make reading an integral and enjoyable part of your daily life.

Weaving the Tapestry - How to Apply This in Daily Life

Theory is meaningless without application. Here is how to integrate this entire system into the reality of your work, studies, and personal time.

The Daily Reading Diet: A Practical Blueprint

Recognize that not all reading is created equal. You will use different gears of your reading engine for different materials.

1st **Gear (The Survey Scan - 5-10 minutes):** For emails, news articles, reports, and blog posts.

Technique: Aggressive previewing. Read the subject line, first paragraph, subheadings, bullet points, and concluding sentence. Use a pacer to zip through. Your goal is to extract the core message and decide if it requires a deeper read or an action.

Outcome: You process vast amounts of information quickly, triaging your attention effectively and avoiding the "read everything in detail" trap.

2nd Gear (The Analytical Read - 15-30 minute Pomodoros): For professional documents, academic papers, complex articles, and non-fiction books.

Technique: The full system. Pre-read to build your scaffold. Set your purpose. Use your pacer in chunking mode. Stay active with a highlighter or margin notes. Pause after sections to mentally summarize. Apply the 20-20-20 rule religiously.

Outcome: You achieve deep comprehension and strong retention of important material, making you more effective and knowledgeable in your field.

3rd Gear (The Immersive Read - For pleasure and literary depth): For novels, memoirs, and poetry.

Technique: Here, speed is often secondary to savoring. You may slow down to appreciate language, imagery, and character development. However, your trained skills prevent your mind from wandering. You maintain a strong flow state, and you can use your expanded vision to take in beautiful descriptive passages in sweeping gulps rather than small sips. You read for enjoyment, but with unparalleled focus.

Outcome: A deeper, more immersive, and more satisfying experience with literature, free from the fatigue that once might have cut your reading sessions short.

The Weekly Habit:

Protect Your Time: Schedule your 2nd Gear reading sessions into your calendar like any other important appointment.

Curate Your Input: Use your scanning skills to quickly assess articles and books, choosing only the best to dedicate your deep reading time to.

Review and Synthesize: Spend 15 minutes at the end of the week glancing over your notes and summaries. This reinforces the knowledge and demonstrates the tangible value of your practice.

The Never-Ending Story - Becoming a Lifelong Learner

Finally, we must look beyond the mechanics to the ultimate purpose. The goal was never just to "read fast." The goal was to become a different person—a more empowered, confident, and perpetual learner.

Final Motivation: The Compound Interest of the Mind

Think of every book you read, every article you analyze, every new idea you synthesize as a deposit into the bank account of your mind. At first, the individual deposits seem small. But with consistent practice, the compound interest is staggering.

You will develop Intellectual Confidence: You will no longer feel overwhelmed by dense material or a large reading list. You will approach challenges with the quiet confidence of someone who has a proven system to dissect and understand anything put in front of them.

You will make Unexpected Connections: The wider and deeper you read, the more your knowledge becomes a interconnected web. An idea from a history book will solve a problem at work. A concept from a novel will provide a metaphor for a personal challenge. You will see the world not in isolated fragments, but as a rich, complex tapestry.

You will never be bored or stagnant: A lifelong reader has a perpetual source of stimulation, growth, and companionship. There is always a new world to explore, a new skill to learn, a new perspective to understand. This practice is the ultimate antidote to intellectual stagnation.

You will leave a legacy of wisdom: The knowledge you acquire and integrate shapes your decisions, your character, and your conversations. It makes you a more interesting partner, a more insightful friend, a more visionary leader, and a wiser human being. This is the true ROI of your investment.

Your journey as a reader did not end with this book; it has just been重新装备 (re-equipped) and重新启动 (re-launched). You have the tools. You have the system. You have the understanding.

Now, go and read.

Read to learn. Read to grow. Read to escape. Read to connect. Read with speed, but more importantly, read with purpose. The world of ideas is waiting for you, and you are now perfectly equipped to explore it all.

This is not the end. This is your new beginning.